Psychotherapy
A Personal Approach

Psychotherapy
A Personal Approach

D. J. Smail

J. M. Dent & Sons Ltd
London, Melbourne and Toronto

First published 1978
© D. J. Smail 1978

Printed in Great Britain by
Biddles Ltd, Guildford, Surrey
and bound at the
Aldine Press, Letchworth, Herts
for
J. M. Dent & Sons Ltd,
Aldine House, Albemarle Street, London

This book is set in 10 on 12pt Compugraphic English

British Library Cataloguing in Publication Data
Smail, David John
    Psychotherapy.
    1.Psychotherapy
    I. Title
    616.8'914   RC480

    ISBN 0-460-12027-1

Contents

Acknowledgments

The author and publisher wish to thank the following for permission to reproduce copyright material:

Feyerabend, P. To New Left Books for an extract from *Against Method* (1975).

Fingarette, H. To Routledge and Kegan Paul Ltd and Humanities Press for an extract from *Self-Deception* (1969).

Freud, S. For an extract from 'The Unconscious', to the Hogarth Press Ltd (*Standard Edition of the Complete Psychological Works of Sigmund Freud*, 1915. Trans. and ed. James Strachey. Vol. XIV) and to Basic Books, Inc. (*The Collected Papers of Sigmund Freud*, Vol. IV, edited by Ernest Jones, M.D., authorized translation under the supervision of Joan Riviere, published by Basic Books, Inc., Publishers, New York, by arrangement with the Hogarth Press Ltd and the Institute of Psycho-Analysis, London).

For an extract from 'Femininity' to the Hogarth Press Ltd (*Standard Edition*, Vol. XXII) and to W. W. Norton, Inc. (*New Introductory Lectures on Psychoanalysis*, 1965).

Hayek, F. A. To the Hutchinson Publishing Group Ltd and Random House, Inc., for extracts from 'The Primacy of the Abstract' in A. Koestler and J. R. Smythies (eds.) *Beyond Reductionism* (1972).

Jung, C. G. To Routledge and Kegan Paul Ltd and Princeton University Press for extracts from *The Practice of Psychotherapy* (1954).

Koch, S. To the *Journal of Humanistic Psychology* for an extract from 'The Image of Man Implicit in Encounter Group Therapy' (Fall 1971).

Landfield, A. W. To John Wiley and Sons Ltd, for an extract from the chapter by Landfield in D. Bannister (ed.) *Issues and Approaches in the Psychological Therapies* (1975).

Polanyi, M. To Routledge and Kegan Paul Ltd and University of Chicago Press for an extract from *Personal Knowledge* (1958).

Sartre, J.-P. To Methuen and Co. Ltd and Librairie Gallimard, and to Philosophical Library, Inc., for extracts from *Being and Nothingness*. Reprinted by permission of Philosophical Library, Inc. Copyright © 1956 by Philosophical Library, Inc.

1

The Context of Psychotherapy

There tends to be a certain mystique surrounding psychotherapy. This often occasions in the uninitiated that attitude of almost reluctant reverence—easily turning to derision—which is usually to be found in situations in which we invest others (priests, gurus, doctors) with powers and abilities more advanced than our own. With some notable exceptions, psychotherapists themselves have done little to puncture this mystique, and indeed many continue to further by all means possible an image of themselves as expert technicians in the alteration of human behaviour and psychological suffering, or as possessors of some kind of ultimate knowledge of how human beings should be, and how to get them to-be it.

Our culture is saturated through and through with beliefs about human nature and society which provide a rich nutrient on which the psychotherapy industry can feed. Men and women should be happy—anxiety, depression, fear, panic and confusion are in no way acceptable, and, where they do arise, are to be banished as quickly as possible from the psychological scene. People must be *competent* to achieve those—largely materialistic—aims which fall within the range of possibilities determined by their social position. People must *get on with* other people. Love is good and hate is terrible. People must be sexually 'adjusted' and must *enjoy* sex. Families must be harmonious. People must find out what their 'full potential' as human beings is, and then realize it. People by and large cannot help the way they are: they are moulded by genetic endowment, the physical world and their relations (particularly in childhood) with others. You need an expert to see what's gone wrong and to put it right.

The experts, certainly, are ready and waiting, and the credibility of their role is immeasurably reinforced by the confidence in its own institutions our society generates. Social institutions, indeed, are often scarcely seen as human creations, and hardly at all as the frail and fallible, transitory structures they are. They are seen rather as enduring *realities*, as tangible proof of the correctness of our social

1

vision, as validations of our ideas about our own nature and conduct. And the claims to expertise of our experts are upheld by the very fact that they hold a position in the institutional network. For example, the very existence of schools and universities, professional teachers' organizations, hierarchies of academic rank, and so on, tends to be taken by all but a handful of critics as a kind of tacit justification of our fundamental ideas about the nature of education (e.g. that knowledge is *taught to* pupils by teachers).

This kind of attitude is well exemplified by the remarks of a student psychiatric nurse which demonstrated her readiness to abandon her own experience in the face of institutional disconfirmation. Her impression of her patients was that their problems stemmed from social and material difficulties, but not from illness; but they *must* be ill, she concluded, 'otherwise they wouldn't be in hospital'. Obviously absurd, you might think, and representative of a kind of thinking scarcely worthy of consideration as a serious component in the formation of most people's attitudes. And yet, look at the institution of 'training' and the ready acceptance given by even the most discriminating in our society to 'trained' experts. Just as the fact that somebody is in hospital means that he must be ill, the fact that somebody is trained means that respectable procedures must exist in which to have trained him. As long as your teacher, lawyer, doctor, psychotherapist has satisfactorily emerged from an official training, you can accept that he knows something worth knowing, something which gives him some kind of special authority to interpret the realities of his subject more competently than others. And yet no more than three-quarters of a century ago physicians, no less respected then than in the present day, were on the whole, despite their training, likely to achieve little more than a somewhat swifter demise for their weaker patients than might have occurred without their ministrations. (There are, of course, those who argue that in fact the situation is not so different today.[1])

The point, anyway, is that, not always wisely, we accept a great deal from our experts on trust. I do not want to suggest that there is ultimately anything very much else we can do, but I do want to examine upon what, in the field of psychotherapy, that trust can be based, and above all I hope that, by means of such an examination, the nature of psychotherapy and the character of its practitioners can be rendered a good deal less mysterious.

The nature of psychotherapy has not been determined by scientific insights into the objective realities of human functioning.

Nor could it be. It has on the whole been determined by a somewhat incoherent mixture of assumptions about what constitutes human health and happiness, combined with ideas about how one person can set about understanding, influencing and changing others. It is with these assumptions and ideas that this book will be centrally concerned, offering criticism as well as alternative conceptions.

The first task in this enterprise is to attempt an initial understanding of what is meant by 'psychotherapy', and to indicate the particular areas of our interest.

There is, in fact, no such thing as 'psychotherapy', and to assume that there is is to make a mistake which, as we shall see later, has in the past caused a good deal of misunderstanding about the nature and value of psychological methods of treatment. The field loosely covered by the term 'psychotherapy' comprises, on the contrary, a wide range of philosophies, theories and techniques which are frequently in marked opposition to each other, and are defended and attacked from deeply entrenched, and contrasting, ideological positions. A closer look at some of these positions will be taken in the next chapter. For the moment we should note that 'psychotherapy' can range from the intricate and closely woven theories of human personality and mental functioning which led Sigmund Freud and his followers to develop the techniques of psychoanalysis, to brief commonsensical chats between medical practitioners and their patients ('supportive psychotherapy') which consist of little more than sympathetic listening and more-or-less considered advice. The aims of 'psychotherapy' can vary between the 'cure' of neurotic or other disturbances in individuals thought to be mentally ill, and the acquisition by mentally well-adapted and socially successful people of heightened states of self-awareness, 'transpersonal conscious-ness', 'individuation', and so on. The theoretical mechanisms of change which psychological therapists postulate to account for their practical activities can similarly vary from the operation of unconscious mental dynamics, to the conditioning of physiological reflexes, to which latter process the 'mind' is thought to be irrelevant. Psychotherapists may claim to be able to treat people individually, in families, in groups, or even by correspondence course. The arena could be a mental hospital, a private consulting room, your own home, a 'growth centre' for week-end 'encounters', or almost anywhere else. Psychotherapists themselves may be medically trained psychiatrists, psychologists (who do not have medical qualifications), social workers, or in general any of a wide range of people to be found in the 'helping professions'; or they may be people who have trained in some particular psychotherapeutic creed without any other basic training, lay counsellors, or simply people who have bestowed upon themselves the title 'psychotherapist' and nailed a brass plate to their front door.

Faced with such divergence, we shall for the purposes of this book inevitably have to be selective. Most of the serious thinking and research which has gone on in the field of psychotherapy has been in the context of the treatment of mental disorder, and that mainly concerned with so-called neurotic illness. Recent years have seen an explosion in the 'growth', 'humanistic', and 'encounter' approaches which often concentrate more on ideals of human psychological functioning than on the removal of neurotic symptoms. While we cannot afford to ignore the latter, we shall concentrate mainly on the former: because it is here that the issues concerning psychological disturbance, its causes and its treatment, are in sharpest relief; because this, at the present time at least, is the area of greater social significance; and, not least, because it is in this area that my own experience has largely been acquired.

It is not my intention in this book simply to educate the interested reader—even if I could—in the current status and background of psychological therapies, to put him or her in touch, as it were, with the most advanced thinking on the subject, or to offer a privileged insight into recent developments of the medico-psychological and social/behavioural sciences. On the whole, as already suggested, we tend to approach the subject-matter of our intellectual and scientific institutions with reverence, in the tacit belief that the very most we could hope to achieve would be to *learn from* them. In the case of psychological theories and therapies, the natural tendency to accept what experts say as valid (or at least as *more* valid than one's own opinion) is reinforced by the enormous prestige that medicine and science command in our culture—and it is in medicine and science that most psychotherapies claim to have their roots. Science and medicine are endowed—and not only in the popular conception, but by many medics and scientists—with an *authority* which rivals that of mediaeval scholastic theology. It is my view, and one which I shall attempt to elaborate later, that this authority is ill founded, and indeed its acceptance perverts the development of human knowledge and undermines human experience. However this may be, what does seem absolutely clear to me is that, as things stand at present, the more or less *unquestioning* acceptance of the intellectual respectability, scientific soundness and clinical value of any of the psychological therapies cannot be justified on any grounds. For this reason, then, I feel that educating (or training) a person in 'psychotherapy' is not enough: such an approach could, and indeed does, (a) result in the creation of 'experts', semi-experts and technologists who promulgate theories or apply therapeutic techniques with very little critical understanding of the dubious nature of their conceptual foundations, and (b) reinforce a cultural attitude in which, in matters with which they are not acquainted at first hand, people simply accept what they find.

It is surely not possible for any disinterested observer to survey the contemporary scene in psychotherapy without, at least, bewilderment, or, at most, despair. There are so many approaches, so many competing claims, such differing appeals to scientific or moral authority, that we cannot simply take what we find and hope that sense will emerge from it all in the course of time. We have no alternative but to return at some stage to first principles, to examine critically the scientific and moral ideologies which underpin psychotherapy in its many forms.

In the course of this book, then, I shall be very critical of many current approaches to psychotherapy, and, in advocating the substitution of currently dominant conceptions of medical and scientific authority with the authority of the *personal* experience of those involved in psychotherapy (to be elaborated in later chapters), if I do not lay myself open to charges of mindless iconoclasm, I am at least likely to incur the displeasure of much of the psychotherapy 'establishment'. This is unfortunate, but the risk must be taken.

Since the central focus of this book is to be theory and practice in the psychotherapeutic treatment of neurosis, it is necessary at this stage to sketch in the general background in which such treatment takes place.

Although psychotherapy has its roots in medicine, most modern psychotherapies are in many respects opposed to purely medical approaches to mental or behavioural disorders: few psychotherapists, for example, would believe that the main causes of neurosis are physiological, but would see them rather as residing in the individual's acquired experience. Psychotherapy, again, is not, in Britain at least, the dominant approach to the treatment even of purely neurotic disorders (this would not so much be the case in the United States). The anxieties, phobias, obsessions and depressions which are held to constitute the symptoms of neurosis are most frequently treated by the use of tranquillizing and anti-depressive drugs, and the medically trained psychiatrists who prescribe such treatment see themselves most frequently as physicians, whose primary approach to the alteration of behaviour is via the body. It is perhaps true that few psychiatrists would claim that the neuroses are primarily physical disorders, and most would pay lip-service to the 'influence of the environment'. This passing acknowledgment of environmental influence does not, however, alter the fact that the treatment they offer is most often exclusively physical in nature. The sheer extent of the problem of psychological disturbance coupled with the fundamentally medical nature of psychiatry means that, in the British National Health Service, psychotherapy is hard to come by, and where it is to be found, tends to be reserved for the more articulate and middle-class patients for whom research on the whole suggests it is most useful. Outside the context of the National Health Service, psychotherapy is often, though not always, a lengthy and expensive business, and its patients are far more likely to be found among an affluent middle class than elsewhere. In America, psychotherapy is seen as a more integral part of psychiatry, and this, combined with a much greater commitment to private practice, means that it is more readily available. However, it is important to realize that, in a global context, psychotherapy as an approach to psychological suffering plays only a very minor role, and is largely restricted to the more socially privileged sections of society.

Despite its opposition, in many respects, to medicine, it is important to examine the legacy which psychotherapy has inherited from it, and the influence that medical assumptions have had on psychotherapeutic approaches. Some of that inheritance will already have become apparent in the early pages of this book: so far I have been using terms like 'treatment', 'neurosis', 'patient' largely uncritically, except for some use of inverted commas or qualifying clauses. These are, of course, terms which make no attempt to hide their medical origins. This is not the place to document the process by which medicine made the field of psychological disturbance its own—others, like Thomas Szasz, have done so very satisfactorily:[2] it may for our purposes be sufficient to note that the founding fathers of psychotherapy and their intellectual mentors were doctors, and were imbued with an unshakable confidence in the conceptions of medical science prevalent at the end of the last century. You do not, for example, have to explore the writings of Sigmund Freud very far before stumbling across the most sweeping—indeed arrogant— assertions of the intellectually unassailable nature of mechanistic scientific inquiry and its primacy over all other forms of human spiritual endeavour.

Thus, a system of classifying psychological problems was rapidly constructed which reflected approaches which had proved useful in physical medicine, and the relation of the sufferer to his sufferings was modelled on the relation of the patient to his symptoms. Even today, psychiatry has little hesitation in characterizing psychological disturbance as 'mental illness', and indeed we are encouraged by the medical profession and the health authorities to think of mental illnesses as 'illnesses like any other'. Partly, no doubt, some of the impetus behind this campaign is humanitarian, and it may be feared that the alternative to regarding somebody as mentally ill is to regard him as in some way intrinsically evil, stupid, or *responsible* for his condition.

There has been much criticism in recent years of the concept of mental illness (the main critic being Thomas Szasz, whose major work has already been referred to), yet nevertheless the concept has become deeply and concretely embedded in our society, and shows no signs of becoming less so. Psychological disturbance is mental *illness*, it is *treated* in *outpatient clinics* or mental *hospitals*, by *doctors* and mental *nurses*. The methods of treatment are, as already pointed out, largely physical in nature: mainly drugs, but also electro-convulsive therapy, which necessitates a general anaesthetic, and even brain surgery. Psychological disorder has given rise, in short, to a gigantic medical and pharmacological industry. For this reason alone it takes considerable nerve to suggest that alternative views of psychological disorder are possible.

In many respects it is towards alternative views that psychotherapy, in its various versions, points. Many therapists, for instance, reject at least some of the terminology of medicine—they prefer to speak, for example, of 'clients' rather than 'patients'. Most psychotherapists have little or nothing to do with physical treatments, and prefer to see their clients as far as possible outside medical settings such as hospitals and clinics. Some forms of psychological treatment have their theoretical roots in entirely non-medical disciplines: those techniques loosely grouped under the heading 'behaviour therapy', for example, draw their inspiration from experimental psychology and the study of learning, although most have accepted to some extent the diagnostic classification built by the early psychiatrists and psychoanalysts.

It is hoped that it will prove possible in this book to crystallize an alternative to the dominant medical approach to psychological suffering, and to highlight those aspects of psychotherapeutic thinking which help us to do so. The task will be, then, to provide an account of how somebody can be 'neurotic' without being ill, stupid, evil or deliberately wayward. Our task will, however, be made doubly difficult by the additional contention that, while being none of these things, the neurotic individual is also *not helpless.*

So far I have betrayed clearly enough my objection to the medical approach, but I have not made clear the reason for that objection. It lies, in fact, precisely in the centrality to the illness conception of the *helplessness* of the person supposed to be mentally ill. The medical approach is par excellence a *mechanistic* approach to psychological disturbance: it characterizes the patient as a passive, helpless mechanism, whose only hope for recovery lies in the expert readjustment of the faulty parts.

In the first place, I object to this view because it seems to me simply to be wrong, and in later chapters I shall try to persuade the reader also that it is wrong. Second, because it is wrong, the view of man as helpless mechanism seems to me to have disastrous consequences. From a general point of view it generates social institutions which are designed to organize, manipulate and mould people to *institutional* ends and obscures from them that they can manipulate social institutions to their own ends. From a specific point of view it has the result that the psychologically disturbed individual is denied, at least from the viewpoint of 'official' theory, the one most effective avenue to coping with his disturbance, i.e. helping himself. In practical terms, this most often means that he is left to fester psychologically in his fears, confusions and painful personal relations, while somebody tinkers with his body chemistry or stuns him periodically with electric shocks. Patients in the average mental hospital are *dis*couraged from facing their psychological problems or questioning the values of the (usually) benevolently authoritarian régime which takes them in its charge and claims responsibility for their future psychological health. The patient is thus denied access to the means of helping himself, or at least his access to it is discouraged. For, to help himself, he must be able to examine, understand and change his psychological predicament. He may indeed need help in doing this, but that help will certainly not consist in diverting his attention from his predicament.

It is of course in this area that the psychotherapies hold out their promise. Superficially, at least, they seem to offer ways in which the individual can come to an understanding of his predicament and in which the predicament itself can be changed. And indeed it will be an argument of this book that from the psychotherapies can be distilled a way of conceptualizing how the individual can take charge of his own psychological functioning even when subjectively at his most helpless and 'ill'.

And yet, if psychotherapies hold out hope of achieving such a liberating view of man and his psychological problems, it is often in the teeth of their own theoretical leanings. If psychotherapy has escaped from some of the more limiting medical assumptions touched on above, it still in large part shares with medicine about the most limiting assumption of all: that is, the assumption of mechanism. Psychotherapists of many, though not all, persuasions tend to have taken over unthinkingly the view common to early medicine and academic psychology that to be scientific you have to accept some mechanistic (though they might not actually use the word) constraints. The acceptance of some form of determinism, for example, is widespread among psychotherapists, and indeed is as central to psychoanalysis as it is to behavioural psychotherapy. Similarly, the doctor-patient, expert repairer-faulty machine relationship is characteristic of many forms of psychotherapy. Where therapists have departed from these models, they have often done so hesitantly and nervously—making ritual obeisance to determinism, perhaps, by speaking of the patient's 'sense of mastery' rather than his freedom, and so on. In the next chapter the theoretical background of some of the major psychotherapies will be examined in much greater detail, and later in the book we shall hope to provide reasons for therapists to make the break from mechanistic assumptions more boldly. But it is important at this stage to note one particular consequence of the insidious invasion of psychotherapy by medico-scientific mechanism: namely, that even psychotherapists run into conceptual difficulties when they try to help patients with their helplessness.

Most patients—and certainly those who fall into the 'neurotic' class with which we are mainly concerned—come to the therapeutic situation equipped with a theory, or theories, about themselves which are not so different from those of the professional experts. Partly because of the expectations engendered by our culture and its social institutions, and partly because it is the most *convenient* belief for them to hold (since the unacceptable alternatives seem to be malice or stupidity), patients tend to see their psychological problems as outside their own control. They may find themselves in the grip of behaviours they seem unable to resist—for example, compulsions to keep clean and free of various kinds of contamination, or an irresistible urge to engage in repetitive checking that they have not committed some careless and potentially dangerous act; or they may feel unaccountably assailed by apparently baseless feelings of anxiety or panic; or such intense fears of apparently harmless objects or situations that they have to organize their lives round avoiding them. Or they may feel a pervasive depression and lack of interest in life without being able to identify its source; or perhaps an inability sexually to consummate an otherwise apparently satisfactory relationship. The complaints, in fact, which people bring to their doctor or therapist can vary over an almost infinite range—from being compelled to eat coal to feeling sexually attracted to horses—but they tend to have in common that the person feels at their mercy and unable to help himself. The theory a patient holds, tacitly or explicitly, to account for his predicament may appeal to a mechanical disorder of his body, a childhood trauma, financial problems or stresses at work, the malice of others, and so on; and in this he may find a ready echo in the theoretical beliefs of his therapist. Everything, including the very fact that his therapist *exists* as a socially accredited expert in his problems, suggests to the patient that he may submit himself to the therapist much as the host of appendicitis submits himself to the surgeon. Yet he will soon discover that, far from being the passive recipient of various technical procedures, he is engaged in a taxing struggle with his problems which makes great demands on his personal, active resources. The therapist also, while embodying the role of technical expert, will in fact (and possibly with an uncomfortable recognition of the dimly implied contradiction) be making demands upon his patient's resources, and requiring of him his active participation in treatment.

This is one of the most puzzling and difficult of the theoretical problems which psychotherapy has to deal with, and one which may well cause the patient a lot of grief. He is encouraged by the mechanistic temper of the age to look for 'the cause' of his psychological problems. He no more knows why he is neurotic than I know why I am a psychologist, but the bits and pieces of popular medicine or psychoanalysis he has picked up will set him off in a diligent search for causal events, childhood experiences, etc., which he expects to 'explain' his condition, which in turn, having been explained, will presumably vanish. It may well become a source of anxiety, and even anger to him to discover that this approach proves fruitless, and it only confuses and further angers him that his therapist, while professing beliefs which apparently support his mechanistic strategies, in actuality seems to be demanding of him something else. We are here anticipating themes which will be developed in greater detail at a later stage. We can note, however, that the anxiety, anger and confusion which tends to arise in this situation frequently results in patients' terminating psychotherapy and departing in disgust or despair, thereby adding to the statistics which demonstrate that, whatever else it is (and it is much else!) psychotherapy is not a sure-fire technical method of curing 'neurotic illness'.

Much of the language, and some of the concepts, which the medical approach has contributed to the understanding of psychological disturbance is hard to dispense with without artificiality. The terms 'neurosis', 'treatment', 'patient', and indeed 'therapy' itself, as well as many others, cannot easily be separated from their medical connotations, and tend almost unavoidably to foster mechanistic assumptions about the nature of psychotherapy. The dilemma of the writer who wishes, as I do, to reject these assumptions without straining the reader's patience by inventing an entirely new vocabulary is not easily solved. 'Neurosis', if it can be thought of without the implication it carries of being a medical diagnosis, a type of disease entity, can be usefully retained as a shorthand to describe a kind of strategy by which a person can deceive himself about the reasons for and aims of his conduct (a view to be elaborated later). If I could think of an equally succinct term which expressed what I mean and carried no medical implications, I should use it. Since I cannot, I shall continue to use the term in the slightly idiosyncratic sense given above, and hope that I am not too frequently misunderstood. The substitution of 'client' for 'patient' now frequently made by psychotherapists I do not myself feel to be particularly satisfactory. It is true that 'client' avoids the directly medical flavour of 'patient', but it does not escape—indeed it in some ways furthers—a view of the therapeutic relationship as one of professional expert and passive recipient. Further, while being in this respect no less mystifying and mechanizing than 'patient', it introduces a commercial tone to the therapeutic 'transaction' which, though many therapists feel the commercial aspect to be of central (rather than incidental) importance to therapeutic effectiveness, I for one find mildly unfortunate. Because of this, and because the repetitive use of the words 'person' or 'individual' tends to become irritating after a time, though basically I prefer them, I shall not shrink from using the familiar 'patient'. 'Treatment', 'therapy', and so on, could I think be more usefully, and accurately, called something like 'psychological guidance' or simply 'help', but here again to do so single-mindedly would inevitably seem artificial. In time perhaps the context in which these words are used will establish their detachment from medicine and medical assumptions, and their presence in the language will depend simply on their convenience. That, anyway, is why I use them. I shall certainly *not* be talking about 'mental illness'.

1 Illich, Ivan. (1975). *Medical Nemesis*. London: Calder & Boyars.
2 Szasz, T. (1962). *The Myth of Mental Illness*. London: Secker & Warburg.

2

Approaches to Psychotherapy

The approaches to therapy to be discussed in this chapter have been selected first for their general importance and influence, and secondly because they exemplify in one way or another theoretical, or even ideological positions which it is our aim to understand and make explicit. It is not the purpose of this book to provide a comprehensive review of the various kinds of psychotherapy practised today, or a full history of their development. The reader looking for this kind of information should consult one of the texts already available which are aimed at fulfilling this purpose.[1] There is a particular class of approaches to psychotherapy—those involving groups of patients, families and marital couples—which I shall not be considering in this chapter. Their omission reflects a concern for economy of space and, more cogently perhaps, my belief that the central issues in psychotherapy can be raised by a consideration of individual therapy alone; it does not, however, carry any implication of relative therapeutic unimportance for these methods, many of which have great potential usefulness.

It is important to emphasize that in this chapter I am considering therapy from the point of view of what therapists *say* they do, and not from that of what they *do* do. In other words, my perspective is theoretical. As we shall see in Chapter 3, it is by no means the case that what therapists say they do always matches or describes accurately what they actually do. In that case, it may be asked, why concentrate on a theoretical perspective? Why not just describe what actually happens in therapy? My reason is that, though theories are often not (indeed, in some cases because of their fundamental absurdity *could* not be) put into therapeutic practice, they nevertheless have consequences for our view of ourselves and our relations with each other which are very far-reaching. I hope to demonstrate this later in this chapter.

One cannot, then, afford to ignore theory, however much it departs from practice, and however much practitioners may feel contemptuous of it. Ours is becoming a largely technological, rather than a scientific, culture. We are concerned with *whether* things 'work', not with how and why they do; we are more concerned with cost-effectiveness than with truth. In the field of psychotherapy this leads, particularly in some camps, to a Philistine dismissal of theoretical considerations; what matters to these therapists is simply whether or not the patient 'gets better'. It so happens that many of the therapists of this persuasion belong to the 'behaviour therapy' school (to be discussed below), which in origin springs from a theoretical position which is very easily demolished. Despite behavioural theory being in ruins, behavioural therapeutic technologists will happily carry on, because they believe that what they are doing 'works'. If you attack their theoretical position, as it is so easy to do, they will accuse you of attacking a straw man, gaining a hollow victory, etc., as they no longer really subscribe to that, or any other, theory. This would be all very well if it were not for the fact that the theory has not been abandoned at all, but carries on under cover, so to speak. For in the field of psychotherapy, in which by adopting some criterion or other of human health or happiness the therapist is putting forward *values*, he simply cannot escape having a theory about human nature and what is good for it. There is just no way of saying whether a patient is 'better' without having a theory about how people ought to *be*, any more than there is a way of trying to change people without having a theory about how to do it. The fact that therapists exist who are unaware of their therapeutic theory is considerably more frightening than the existence of therapists who consciously subscribe to a theory which is, for example, absurd or self-contradictory. The latter, at least, are answerable for their values, while the former promulgate theirs without knowing what they are. This is no merely abstract intellectual problem, as we shall see shortly.

Psychotherapy as a formal procedure appealing for its justification to the accepted principles of science has its origins in Freud's psychoanalysis. Psychotherapy is of course not to be confused with psychoanalysis: the former is a much broader term than the latter, which refers specifically to the theoretical beliefs and therapeutic practices of Freud and his followers.

Most of the many variants of psychotherapy have moved very far indeed from psychoanalysis, and in not many of them would it now be felt that they owed all that much to it. There are also, certainly, many more psychotherapists—of various persuasions—than there are psychoanalysts, and there is little doubt that psychoanalysis is no longer the power it once was in this field. But although 'pure culture' psychoanalysts may be relatively thin on the ground nowadays, Freud's ideas have had an enormous impact on our culture, and in the public mind Freudian analysis is often more or less synonymous with psychotherapy. In fact, in the professional spheres of psychiatry and psychology, Freudian psychoanalysis has probably had less influence than outside, but even so there can be few areas of professional concern which have not at least been touched by some aspect of Freud's thought.

It would be both arrogant and foolish to attempt to condense an adequate account of psychoanalysis into the space available in this chapter, but perhaps enough can be said to convey the general tenor of some of the debates within psychoanalysis and to indicate to the reader where further information might be found.[2]

The range and extent of Freud's output was vast. Among other things, he bequeathed to posterity a theory of the development of personality, a theory of psychological (mental) functioning, and a theory of neurosis together with a technique for its treatment. None of these would today be accepted without qualification by any but a small handful of highly orthodox psychoanalysts, but in the course of developing his position Freud elaborated a number of technical concepts which are still extremely influential.

Freud subscribed to a brand of mechanistic rationalism which was in his day thought by many to be characteristic of science, and he saw the 'discoveries' of psychoanalysis as opening the way to a more or less final understanding of the nature of man. Human nature could thus be *reduced* to a relatively small set of mechanisms, the nature of which it was the business of psychoanalysis to reveal. In this way, man could in principle be scientifically understood as an *object*, in much the same way as physical objects could be understood by the natural sciences. From this alone it is possible to appreciate how easily a mystique could come to be attached to psychoanalysis: the analyst becomes a subject whose knowledge encompasses and explains the conduct of those objects—people—to whom he turns his attention. Despite a certain mock modesty, it is evident from much of Freud's writing that to a great extent he revelled in this mystique.

One could caricature Freud's conception of psychological functioning as a whole, as a kind of vast steam engine, in which the motive power of 'libido'—sexual and aggressive energy—is forced through various valves (defence mechanisms) and chambers (levels of consciousness) until it is finally converted into observable activity. In many respects Freud does seem to have had this kind of model in mind. Behaviour is indeed reduced in the end to the way the individual has managed to deal with his sexual and aggressive energy, from the early vicissitudes of breast feeding and toilet training (the famous oral and anal stages of infantile development) to the full flowering of genital sexuality, not to mention the enormous challenge of the Oedipal stage, at which the child has to cope with the threats posed by its sexual attraction to its parent of opposite sex. All later development, and in particular the formation of neurotic symptoms, was seen as hinging on the conscious and unconscious manoeuvres which were brought to bear in the attempted resolution of these sexual problems. In some ways the individual was seen as the embodiment of a moral struggle between the opposing forces of his psyche, his unconscious, preconscious and conscious minds providing the arena for battles between his 'id' (the naked impulse to sexual and aggressive satisfaction), his 'ego' (roughly corresponding to a consciously aware self) and his 'superego', or conscience. Through psychoanalysis the individual could become aware of some of the unconscious springs of his problems, particularly as these centred in his sexual relations in childhood with his parents, and by working through them and their consequences in his relationship with his analyst, bring them under the conscious control of his ego. Since the problems were deeply rooted in the first place in the unconscious mind, the techniques of psychoanalysis were to focus on ways of reaching this inaccessible stratum. Having tried, and abandoned, hypnosis, Freud concentrated instead on free association and the analysis of dreams. For although the unconscious mind could clearly not be expressed directly by the patient, its influence, Freud felt, could be detected in the unmonitored drift of his associations, and in his dreams, where again the vigilance of conscious censorship was relaxed. The processes by which consciousness tries to exclude what is to it the very threatening nature of the unconscious sexual and aggressive impulses, were elaborated in great technical detail and with considerable sophistication by Freud. These are the defence mechanisms, of which the most important is 'repression', which is best characterized, perhaps, as a kind of intentional forgetting: the individual succeeds either in actively ejecting sexually or aggressively charged material from consciousness, or in preventing its initial entry into consciousness.

The nature of unconscious mental contents could often only be divined from the symbolic distortions they had undergone in dreams or free associations, and for this reason Freud developed what now appears to be a rather simplistic lexicon of symbolism, which, among other things, could be of service in the analyst's 'interpretation' to the patient of the meaning of his unconscious (dream and free-associative) productions. In this sense, the analyst would be able to tell the patient what his thoughts, fantasies and dreams *really meant*. This is a point we shall certainly be returning to, but it is scarcely any wonder that in the early days of psycho-analysis the hint of powers of this kind attracted to it, from some quarters anyway, a quality of almost religious awe.

A central belief of psychoanalysis and many of its later derivatives is that a person's perception of his present relationships—and in particular that with his analyst—is determined unconsciously by his earlier relationship with his parents. The role of the analyst in therapy therefore, at least in part, becomes one of providing a 'screen' onto which the patient can 'project' largely fantasized attributes which betray the psychological structure of his childhood parental relationships. To facilitate this process, the analyst excludes as far as possible any revelation of personal characteristics: he contrives to remain 'neutral'. This is one of the reasons why, in classical psychoanalysis, the analyst sits behind the prone patient, where the latter cannot see him. Feelings the patient has for or about the analyst are thus characterized as the 'transference' onto a neutral figure of qualities which have their origin in the patient's infantile past. The therapist's analysis of this transference, his demonstration to the patient by means of interpretation, etc., of the real significance of the latter's feelings about him, is the central plank in psychoanalytic technique.

There is much in Freud's original formulations which only a tiny minority of his present-day followers would be prepared to defend. His sexual reductionism, for example, cannot, in its more extreme form, command the serious attention of modern psychological theorists. Consider the following quotation from a paper of his on femininity,[3] which, incidentally, makes the modern male chauvinist look like Joan of Arc:

The effect of penis-envy has a share . . . in the physical vanity of women, since they are bound to value their charms more highly as a late compensation for their original sexual inferiority. Shame, which is considered to be a feminine characteristic *par excellence* but is far more a matter of convention than might be supposed, has as its purpose, we believe, concealment of genital deficiency. We are not forgetting that at a later time shame takes on other functions. It seems that women have made few contributions to the discoveries and inventions in the history of civilization;

there is, however, one technique which they may have invented—that of plaiting and weaving. If that is so, we should be tempted to guess the unconscious motive for the achievement. Nature herself would seem to have given the model which this achievement imitates by causing the growth at maturity of the pubic hair that conceals the genitals. The step that remained to be taken lay in making the threads adhere to one another, while on the body they stick into the skin and are only matted together. If you reject this idea as fantastic and regard my belief in the influence of lack of a penis on the configuration of femininity as an *idée fixe*, I am of course defenceless.

However, despite what now appear to be obvious weaknesses in Freud's original ideas, there are many aspects of his elaboration of theory and practice in psychoanalysis which are still highly influential in psychotherapy. If his conception of infantile development in terms of an oversimplified set of crucial psycho-sexual stages has largely been rejected, his formulation of the nature of consciousness (and unconsciousness), repression and other defence mechanisms, has proved to be of fundamental importance.

Freud's view of science committed him to a theory which is, as has been pointed out, reductionist, determinist and mechanistic, and to a view of the therapist's role in analysis as neutral and impersonal. These are features which orthodox psychoanalysis shares with other brands of psychological therapy which place a similar emphasis on the 'scientific' nature of their foundations. It is to orthodox versions of these which we shall turn next, even though chronologically they belong to a much more recent period. We shall return a little later to the variations and developments which have occurred in the broadly psychoanalytic field.

One of the most influential approaches to the treatment of neurosis in the present day is that of 'behaviour therapy'. The theoretical pedigree of behaviour therapy is different from that of psychoanalysis, and it owes little to turn-of-the-century medical thinking. There are perhaps two main theoretical sources of behaviour therapy which can be clearly identified. The first is Pavlov's work in the earlier years of this century on physiological reflexes and the acquisition of conditioned responses in laboratory animals, and the second is the anti-mentalism of J. B. Watson. The development within experimental psychology—largely a pre-occupation of academic institutions—of the tenets of behaviourism, for the origination of which Watson is usually held to be responsible, will be familiar to most readers of this book, and to chronicle them yet again here would be tedious in the extreme. For the uninitiated reader, however, a few words on the scientific ideology of behaviourism might not be out of place.

Behaviourism was a reaction to what many psychologists saw as the hopelessly subjective entanglements into which psychology as an academic discipline had got itself. Disputes over whether people thought with or without the use of visual images, how many instincts could be identified as motivating human behaviour, and so on, made use of techniques of argument and research which seemed uncomfortably distant from those which were being used with such apparent success in the natural sciences. Science, it was felt, must deal only with observables, and the experimental procedures of psychological scientists must be clearly specifiable in terms of what they do, and what the outcome is. If only psychologists could get away from talking about what went on *inside* people (where no one but the subject himself could see—and not even he necessarily reliably) and measure their activity in terms of some *objective* criterion, psychology stood a chance of becoming really scientific. The objective criterion is, of course, behaviour. With great excitement, psychologists discovered that instead of talking about what people felt and thought, which was liable to subjective error, they could talk about, and actually *measure* (quantifiability being another worthy scientific aim) what they *did*. They could then specify their own experimental operations upon the subject (or 'organism', as he came to be called), and measure the result in terms of his reaction. It thus dawned on the behaviourists that you didn't have to talk about 'minds' at all. All pre-scientific, occult nonsense about thoughts, feelings, ideas and purposes could be scrapped and replaced by behavioural responses to experimental stimuli. Here at least was an exact, objective, quantitative psychological science which could, head held high, proclaim that its aim was 'the prediction and control of behaviour'. In place of mind the behaviourists put the reflex arc, which they borrowed from Pavlov. What happens when a human being *learns*, then, is that a behavioural response becomes conditioned to an environmental stimulus. The way it becomes conditioned is through 'reinforcement'; that is, the conditioned reflex between stimulus and response is established through the association of the latter with (usually) reward.

Much of the work of behaviourist psychologists was in the experimental study of learning. Because, for them, consciousness did not exist as a 'scientific' possibility, because the control and manipulation of experimental variables was essential to their model of experimental science, because in general it seemed the easiest thing to do, most of their work in this area was carried out with animals, particularly laboratory rats. A typical learning experiment would thus consist of rewarding an animal by means of food for achieving some goal (such as running correctly through a simple maze) previously determined by the experimenter. Ingenious permutations and manipulations of this basic situation have filled libraries, and the theoretical implications drawn from them held sway in academic psychology for decades. Incredible as it might seem, a view of man without mind, a model of learning built on procedures which, however ingenious, were no more than techniques of training performing animals, seemed an acceptable price to pay for a 'scientific' psychology.

Behaviourism is now no longer the force it once was in academic psychology, but many of its scientific assumptions go marching on, particularly in its psychotherapeutic aspect, i.e. behaviour therapy. Although it is impossible to avoid questioning some of its practical defects, behaviourism has so dominated the psychological scene that psychologists tend to overlook the fact that the behaviourist theoretical principles which they took in with their mother's milk can be equally called into question. Thus, the aims of mechanistic reductionism (to stimulus and response), determinism (which permits 'prediction and control of behaviour') and objectivity still seem self-evidently necessary to many psychologists, and to many of those who are engaged in the treatment of neurosis. The behaviourist's antipathy for 'mentalism' expresses itself among behaviour therapists as a contemptuous hostility towards the ideas of psychoanalysis, with which, as has been said, it otherwise shares rather similar scientific aims. Unseen, unobservable things like unconscious minds are for obvious reasons anathema to the behaviourist.

In their original conception and purest form the techniques of behaviour therapy closely reflect behaviourist scientific ideology. Reasoning from his own, and others', experiments with animal conditioning, Joseph Wolpe, one of the founding fathers of behaviour therapy, concluded that neurotic behaviour was the result of anxiety responses having become conditioned to otherwise neutral stimuli. Due to some quirk in the history of his reinforcement contingencies, the phobic patient, for example, behaves neurotically (anxiously) in the presence of stimuli (e.g. travelling on public transport) which in the normal course of events do not evoke anxiety. The neurosis, therefore, can be understood as no more than its symptoms: one need no longer appeal to the mysterious operation of unconscious complexes or unresolved, and unobservable, sexual conflicts. Remove the symptoms, and you have removed the neurosis. The removal of symptoms is, naturally enough, achieved by the conditioning of a non-anxious response to the offending stimuli. This reasoning gave birth to the technique, widely practised by present-day behaviour therapists, of 'systematic desensitization'. This technique, originally established as viable by Wolpe with cats, relies upon teaching patients to relax, and then conditioning the physical responses of relaxation, which are held to inhibit anxiety, to a graded series of stimuli which represent—often in imagination only—the situations most feared by the patient. Thus the claustrophobic patient, for example, will be asked to imagine, in a relaxed state, a series of situations involving increasing degrees of enclosure or confinement. At the end of the series he will be imagining those situations which in actuality cause him most alarm. If successful, his anxiety will thus be inhibited, and the process of re-conditioning will be complete. The relaxation responses which have been conditioned in imagination will, by the process of 'generalization' (a construct invented by behaviourists to account for the fact that a behavioural response learned in one particular situation will also be evoked in other relevant situations), also obtain in actual, '*in vivo*', situations. Wolpe claimed considerable success for this technique, a point which we shall return to in a later chapter when we come to consider scientific evidence for the efficacy of psychotherapeutic approaches.

'Aversive' techniques of behaviour therapy have also been arrived at on the basis of the conditioning model. In this case punishment (as opposed to the 'positive reinforcement' of reward) has been used to associate an unpleasant, aversive outcome with behaviours which are deemed 'maladaptive'. Deviant sexual behaviour—homosexuality, transvestism, etc.—and alcoholism have been the most frequent targets for this kind of approach. Thus homosexuals may be administered painful electric shocks when they show signs of arousal to homosexual stimuli, or alcoholics are given drugs which react with alcohol and bring about nausea and vomiting.

'Operant conditioning', the brainchild of one of the foremost apologists of behaviourism, B. F. Skinner provides the rationale for a further collection of behaviour therapy techniques (often known as 'behaviour modification', or 'behaviour shaping') which have been widely practised on chronic patients in mental institutions as well as with mentally handicapped or severely disturbed children. In these, reward is made contingent upon 'desirable' behaviours and the absence of reward upon 'undesirable' behaviours. First, an analysis might be made of what an individual patient finds rewarding. This might take the form of sweets, cigarettes, going for a walk, listening to music, having a bath or any one of a number of events or activities. These rewards will then be withheld until the patient 'emits' the behaviour which is to be reinforced (e.g. talking rather than remaining mute, controlling bladder or bowel functions, behaving sociably rather than unsociably, and so on). His behaviour will thus be 'shaped' to acquire new standards of acceptability. The reader who wishes to pursue further the theory and practice of behaviour therapy will find a voluminous literature awaiting him. [4]

As behavioural psychology reduces the person, so behaviour therapy reduces the individual patient to a mindless focus of stimuli and responses, a manipulable object to be predicted, controlled, and shaped to conform to current social norms.

There are crippling objections to behaviourism. Where there is no consciousness, no purpose, there can be no meaning, no values. How can the behaviour therapist *decide* what to do when he is, on his own theory, no more than the helpless result of his reinforcement history—how, indeed, can he account for his own behaviour as subject-scientist when only objectivity is possible? He can only do so, of course, because he shuts his eyes to those aspects of his activity which fail to fit in with his scientific philosophy; he ignores his own experience, distorts that of others, and ends up as a kind of psychological fraud. This is not the place to develop a full critique of behaviourism. That has been done very adequately by others.[5] Although greatly weakening the general acceptance of behaviourism in psychology as a whole, such attacks have not resulted in its total demise. The behaviourist reaction is often simply to shout louder its scientific credo, or, as often in the case of behaviour therapists, to retire into a kind of technological obscurantism which simply insists that, because behaviour therapy works, behavioural theory must be true. To object to behaviourism and its practical applications in terms of its implications for the freedom and dignity of man is liable to meet with sneering accusations of tender-mindedness and an inability to take one's scientific medicine: maybe people are reduced to junction boxes where stimulus meets response, but if that's what science reveals, that's just too bad.

And it is just this question of the *scientific* status of behaviour therapy which seems to mesmerize its proponents, who do not seem to recognize that it is scarcely scientific to hold on to beliefs which contradict fundamental human experience, involve their holders in self-contradiction and fly in the face of rationality. It is by no means my intention to argue here that behaviour therapy techniques do not 'work'—indeed I am convinced that they often do. What the behaviourist cannot provide, and what it seems to me we must earnestly seek, is a theory which explains *why* such techniques work.

For people for whom values are presumably mentalistic cobwebs, behaviour therapists often seem to exude an almost evangelistic zeal:

> The reason for the effectiveness of behaviour modification lies in its derivation from the experimental analysis of behaviour. No other approach in the history of psychology has demonstrated such refined prediction and control over its subject-matter with such scientific rigour, replicability and generality. It should not be surprising therefore that an effective behavioural technology emerges which is based on a powerful science of behaviour.
>
> The cumulative evidence is now sufficient to justify the conclusion that any approach to behaviour change, training, rehabilitation, teaching or education should be informed by operant principles. This means that practical wisdom which many trainers, teachers, rehabilitators and therapists have gathered, with experience in whatever framework they had available to them, can probably be applied more effectively when the laws of behaviour are explicitly recognized and implemented.[6]

But what are we to do with this powerful technology? Who is to decide to what human ills its attentions should be directed? Where at last are we to find a subjective *person* who is able to make decisions of this kind? It may be self-evident that people who don't want to be homosexual shouldn't be, and that a reasonable way of changing them is to ask them to masturbate to pictures of nude men, and electrically shock them when they ejaculate, but how can such self-evidence reveal itself to the blind product of environmental reinforcement? These are questions which cannot be answered by the behaviourist without self-contradiction or sophistry.

In his relationship with his patient, the behaviour therapist, from a purely theoretical point of view, finds himself in the uneasy company of the orthodox psychoanalyst, for, like him, he believes that it is the *technique* of therapy which is important, not the person of the therapist. Whereas the analyst is the vehicle of projected, transference reactions, the behaviour therapist is the scientific technician who juggles stimuli. As long as the juggling is done correctly, the identity of the juggler is immaterial. Many of the early behaviour therapists explicitly espoused this view, and indeed 'automated behaviour therapy', where the therapist is replaced by a machine, is a logical extension of it which some have not shied away from.

Like orthodox psychoanalysis, in short, behaviour therapy has done its level best to remain true to the inspiration of its conception of science. It is reductive, mechanistic, deterministic and impersonal. The practitioners of these forms of psychotherapy are, nevertheless, people, and their saving grace is that what they do in psychotherapy may bear little relation to what they say they do. Unfortunately for them, their conception of what it is to be 'scientific' makes it impossible for them to take into consideration those aspects of their own and their patients' activity which cannot be accommodated within a restricted and simplistic theoretical model. In these as in many other areas of psychology and psychotherapy, we seem in fact to have arrived at a curious inversion of scientific values. If science arose to confront theological dogma with what men actually *experienced*, psychological science these days too often ignores, distorts or denies experience because it does not square with the dogmatic principles of that science.

But by no means all psychotherapists have been afraid to this extent of permitting their personal experience to dictate their theoretical stance. The reductionism and impersonality of Freud's views quickly bred dissent in his own day, and psychoanalysis soon split into a variety of camps representing objections to one or another aspect of the orthodoxy. It is of course not possible fully to document these developments here, but it might be of interest to glance at some of their more salient features.

Carl Jung and Alfred Adler are of course the best known of the dissenters among Freud's contemporaries. Between them, they objected to the sweeping sexual reductionism, as well as the determinism and impersonality of Freud's psychoanalysis, and both formed well-established schools of their own—Jung's 'analytical psychology', and Adler's 'individual psychology'. Neither, however, has had an influence comparable to Freud's on the field of psychotherapy as a whole, although Adler's views had a significant impact in the United States, especially in the area of child guidance.

Adler is probably chiefly remembered for the emphasis he placed on the importance of feelings of inferiority for an understanding of neurosis, and the compensatory activity in which the person engages in order to overcome them. Hence the pomposity of the short man, the verbosity of the stammerer, and so on. In this, of course, can be seen the same kind of reductionism to which Freud appealed. Also, however, Adler placed great emphasis on the individual's *responsibility* for his actions and for changing them: for Adler, thus, the person is no longer solely determined by unconscious forces, but has the opportunity of consciously changing himself and recognizing that his actions are directed towards an end.

Jung was for a time Freud's closest collaborator, and in many ways his conceptual formulations are very similar to Freud's, and no less complex and far-reaching. However, he objected strongly to Freud's all-embracing sexual reductionism, and laid much more emphasis on the spiritual strivings of men to make sense of their lives and to develop fully their individuality. For this reason, a central focus of his interest was on religion and mythology, in which he felt he detected the most fundamental and pervasive of mankind's concerns, and he used his religious and anthropological studies as a basis for the elaboration of a view of the unconscious mind which emphasized the common spiritual foundations of man's experience (the 'collective unconscious'). In focusing in this way on what the person is to make of himself, how he is to grow to self-fulfilment, Jung anticipated by decades some of the present preoccupations of the 'growth movement' in psychotherapy. Jung also reacted to the impersonality of the analyst-patient relationship as conceived by Freud, and chose rather to characterize the situation as follows:

... twist and turn the matter as we may, the relation between doctor and patient remains a personal one within the impersonal framework of professional treatment. By no device can the treatment be anything but the product of mutual influence, in which the whole being of the doctor as well as that of his patient plays its part. . . . For two personalities to meet is like mixing two different chemical substances: if there is any combination at all, both are transformed. In any effective psychological treatment the doctor is bound to influence the patient; but this influence can only take place if the patient has a reciprocal influence on the doctor. You can exert no influence if you are not susceptible to influence. It is futile for the doctor to shield himself from the influence of the patient and to surround himself with a smokescreen of fatherly and professional authority. By so doing he only denies himself the use of a highly important organ of information. The patient influences him unconsciously none the less.[7]

Further, Jung clearly felt uncomfortable with the mechanistic over-generalizations in which many psychoanalysts seemed tempted to engage:

It is enough to drive me to despair that in practical psychology there are no universally valid recipes and rules. There are only individual cases with the most heterogeneous needs and demands—so heterogeneous that we can virtually never know in advance what course a given case will take, for which reason it is better for the doctor to abandon all preconceived opinions. This does not mean that he should throw them overboard, but that in any given case he should use them merely as hypotheses for a possible explanation.[8]

Jung was less interested than either Freud or Adler in the influences upon the individual which determine (or through which he determines) his character, and for elaborations of this area we have to turn to later variants of psychoanalysis.

It soon became apparent that the more or less exclusive focus on a few particularly salient features of infantile development (the oral and anal stages, etc.) was found wanting by thinkers and practitioners in the broad area of psychoanalysis. In America, H. S. Sullivan's 'interpersonal psychiatry', and in Britain Melanie Klein's 'object relations' theory paved the way for a much more minute and exhaustive analysis of the relations between children and those around them, and the mutual influences to which these give rise. Not only is a far wider range of *events* seen as important in influencing the child's development, but also an increasing awareness dawns of the importance of the *meaning* of these events for the individuals in whose world they occur: what is a psychologically significant event in one family may not be in another, this being determined by the construction which is placed upon it by those involved.

This major step in the demechanization of psychoanalysis is matched by changes in the way such theorists tend to view the nature of the relationship between therapist and patient: the child acquires its view of itself in the context of its relations with its parents; that view can be changed only in the context of new relationships, in particular that with the therapist. Thus Guntrip,[9] a modern exponent of the object relations approach, saw the effective factor in psychotherapy as 'not a "technique of treatment" but a "quality of relationship"'. It is interesting to note, however, that, far though they are from Freud's original formulations, there is often still more than a hint of mechanism and determinism to be found in the writings of these therapists. For example Guntrip, in the same paper, wrote that the unconscious 'is the accumulated experience of our entire infancy and early childhood at the hands of the all-powerful adults who formed us. We have no choice about its creation . . .' This formulation ushers onto the scene the psychotherapist in his familiar guise as expert; for the answer, Guntrip felt, is for our culture to become imbued with the findings of depth psychology concerning the 'basic necessities in the personal care of children at all age levels'. He sees hopeful signs that 'this process has already begun in the increasing education of all the social work professions in the principles of psychodynamics'. However, he warns against this being done amateurishly, though 'expertly done it can nip in the bud a tremendous lot of trouble'.

This brief look at some of the developments and divergencies that have occurred in the broad area of psychoanalysis does scant justice to the range and complexity of ideas which are to be found in the literature, and I am aware that there are a number of important themes and people that have not been touched on. However, I hope that this discussion may prove useful in orienting the reader for the later development of themes which have been raised here. But before passing on to consider other major psychotherapeutic schools, we should perhaps pause to reflect upon the changes which have taken place in the sphere of behavioural psychotherapy. In some ways these are parallel to those in psychoanalysis.

Behaviour therapy has not, of course, been on the scene as long as psychoanalysis, and so has not had as long, not only to change, but, more important, to reflect upon its changes and assimilate them theoretically. The major problem which faces the behaviour therapist is how to accommodate changes which are forced upon him by practical experience within a scientific dogma which is woefully inadequate for dealing with them. The close identification of behaviourism with science itself makes this problem particularly acute, for the behaviour therapist cannot simply abandon his behaviourism (discordant as it is with his experience) without risking the loss of his *raison d'être* as a scientist.

The way that some behaviour therapists seem to be coping with this problem is by hanging on to a scientistic behavioural jargon while at the same time quietly shuffling away from the basic principles of behaviourism. Thus, without any reference being made to the familiar mechanics of stimulus and response, conditioned reflex, and so on, 'modelling' will be invoked to explain learning by imitation, and 'cognitive restructuring' may be offered as an acceptable term for what seems to be more or less conventional non-behavioural psychotherapy. In this way the behaviour therapist is able to keep his scientific credentials while abandoning his principles, though not all have been quite as furtive about this as I may have suggested. Lazarus,[10] for example, quite explicitly recognizes that the simplified models of behaviour offered by Wolpe and Skinner have proved inadequate for his therapeutic practices, and this despite the fact that Lazarus himself started out as an enthusiastic conventional behaviourist. Many behaviour therapists are willing now to admit that the nature of the relationship between therapist and patient is of considerable importance to the outcome of treatment, but this once again moves them, potentially, into areas of theoretical complexity which they are ill-equipped to handle. Behaviour therapy can, as has been suggested, carry on quite successfully as a more or less useful collection of treatment procedures, but when such therapists seek to legitimate their activities by an appeal to their scientific foundations, that appeal must be spurious. Still less does the success of their procedures legitimate their theories.

There also exist important schools of psychotherapy, particularly perhaps that of the American psychologist Carl Rogers, which have started out from far less conventional scientific premises than either psychoanalysis or behavioural psychotherapy. Rogers, whose work has had an increasing impact on the whole field of psychotherapy in recent decades, puts forward a view of man as a self-creating, growing individuality who is far from being the helpless victim of deterministic forces or unconscious conflicts. Rogers' views [11] are on the whole optimistic: the man who is open to his own experience and feelings, and those of others, will naturally grow in a psychologically healthy and fulfilling way. If this growth becomes blocked, if for one reason or another he is unable to remain open to his experience, perhaps because it conflicts with some kind of standards he has internalized (so that his 'self' and 'ideal self' are in conflict), then the kind of therapeutic help which will prove most useful to him will be from a therapist who encourages him to trust once again his own potentialities and to allow the natural processes of growth to reassert themselves. Thus therapy becomes a matter of sympathetic, 'non-directive' exploration with the patient of his own experience and its meaning *for him*. Rogerian 'non-directive' or 'client-centred' therapy is quite clear about what the nature of the therapist's role in the therapeutic process should be, and this contrasts sharply with the traditional 'expert mechanic' role we have considered earlier. Far from being there to fit the patient, one way or another, into his own conceptual framework, the Rogerian therapist is there to fit himself in with his client's. The latter will improve by elaborating his own solutions to his own problems in his own way, and the therapist's job is to help him to do so in his own terms, not to impose upon him an irrelevant (to him) psychological system which can only confuse or divert the course of his own experience. With this in mind, Rogers [12] elaborated the conditions he felt necessary and sufficient for therapeutic change, among which were the empathy and genuineness of the therapist, as well as the 'unconditional positive regard' in which he holds the patient. In other words, the therapist must understand the patient *from the latter's viewpoint*, and be able to communicate this understanding to him; he must be a genuine *person* in the relationship, not merely a professional mask; and he must respect and accept the patient warmly and non-judgmentally ('unconditional positive regard' is often shortened simply to 'warmth').

Rogers' work is thus particularly important for its central focus on the *personal* nature of the therapist's involvement in therapy—not, one should note, that this had escaped the notice of Jung and of some other therapists in the more psychoanalytic tradition—and his views probably gained currency through his concern to back them with quantitative research. Being a psychologist himself, not only was he committed to providing some kind of 'hard evidence' for his views, but he also knew what kind of evidence would be countenanced by the social scientists whose background he shared, and it is largely the Rogerian school we have to thank for the impetus which gave rise to much of the research evidence to be discussed in the next chapter.

Rogers quite explicitly rejects mechanism, determinism and reductionism in his psychological theorizing, and yet in developing a view of psychology which will conceptualize man as 'a subjectively free, choosing, responsible architect of self',[13] he still appears to hanker after generalities, seeking 'lawful and orderly relationships' in the 'private worlds of inner personal meanings'. It may be unfair to accuse Rogers, on this evidence, of attempting to subjugate subjectivity by means of the tools of objectivity, or at least of hoping to be able to do so. Nevertheless, there does seem to be something slightly inconsistent about studying subjectivity in order to render it objective in the form of laws which can be 'put to empirical test'. In many ways this kind of inconsistency is even more apparent among some of Rogers' followers. For example, observation of the importance of the therapist's empathy and genuineness in psychotherapy has encouraged some to attempt to *train* therapists to be genuine and empathetic, and thus, inevitably I should have thought, to convert personal qualities into impersonal acquisitions. Again, modern work in the Rogerian field[14] seems to be focusing on a linkage of some of Rogers' ideas with findings from the study of information-processing machines as models of psychological operation. There is of course no reason why this should not be done, except that it seems a strange direction for Rogers' anti-mechanism to take.

There are several schools of psychotherapy which, as with Rogers, emphasize the importance of the individual's own conception of his world and the necessity for taking this as the starting point for understanding him. Some of these are rooted squarely in the tradition of European existentialism, others represent distillations of a number of psychological and philosophical influences into a more or less original theoretical position. The work of Ludwig Binswanger, for example, takes an approach to 'existential analysis' which owes much to, among others, Martin Heidegger. Binswanger's approach is interesting for the thorough-going seriousness with which it treats the patient's subjectivity[15] and attempts to unravel the patient's world in terms of his own meanings. Binswanger's work is, however, almost unknown in Britain, though he has probably had more widespread influence in the United States.

Viktor Frankl is another psychotherapist whose approach—'logotherapy'—owes much to existential philosophy. Frankl, whose influence in the English-speaking world is again largely confined to the United States, makes several points of importance to psychotherapy as a whole which once again demonstrate the contrast between this and more traditional kinds of approach. He is, for example, concerned to stress the *freedom* of the individual and his ultimate responsibility for himself, as well as the importance of an *unself-conscious* kind of engagement with the world. In this latter respect Frankl is to be contrasted with those therapists who have as a central therapeutic aim *increasing* patients' self-awareness. This is a theme which we shall take up in much greater detail later.

Frankl, perhaps because of his long association with the pragmatic culture of the USA, does, despite his existential affiliations, show here and there the same kind of tendency to mechanism which we have already noted in the case of Rogerians. For example, his observation of the disruptive nature of self-consciousness led him to advocate a technique ('paradoxical intention') by means of which the neurotic can disrupt his own neurotic behaviour by trying to perform it deliberately and consciously. In 'logotherapy' and 'paradoxical intention', I am afraid we may be seeing the foundations of yet another of the would-be patented 'systems' with which psychotherapy abounds, making technical claims which contrast sharply with the existential values which are supposed to provide their basis.

The 'personal construct' psychology of George Kelly[16] provides the theoretical backing to a brand of psychotherapy which also stresses the freedom of the person to determine his own nature.

Kelly's basic position bears a strong resemblance to the phenomenological school of philosophy: men build their world out of their personal experience, and the construction arrived at reflects a series of personal choices of ways in which to make sense of immediate experience. In other words, reality is not 'given' to us in some absolute and external sense, but constructed out of the interpretations we place upon our fundamental experience. These interpretations may vary within the individual at different times, and will certainly vary between individuals, since they are operating from different perspectives. Thus there is no single, objective reality, but a variety of constructions of reality which may be more or less satisfactory to the 'construers'. Kelly's is certainly the most profound and sophisticated attempt so far to elaborate the phenomenological position in psychological terms, and his writings have been particularly influential in British social and clinical psychology. It is not possible to do justice to his theoretical views here, but we should not pass on without trying to convey a flavour of the kind of psychotherapy they give rise to.

Since Kelly sees the basic activity of man in terms of his trying, rather in the same way as scientists are acknowledged to do, to make sense of his experience and increase his understanding and control of the events around him, it is not surprising that he likens the therapist-patient situation to that of the scientific research supervisor and his student. Therapy, for the patient, becomes a situation in which he seeks to increase his understanding of his experience and behaviour through reflection and experiment. The therapist's job is to facilitate this process of elaboration and experimentation as best he can. As with the Rogerians, the 'personal construct psychotherapist' will have no fixed idea about how people should *be*, and the course of therapy in this respect will be determined by what the patient believes, and discovers, about himself. In contrast with the Rogerians, however, there is perhaps a little more emphasis on the *technical* nature of the therapist's role (as opposed—though not totally—to its *personal* quality). Since in Kellian psychotherapy the therapist's job is to help the patient investigate, elaborate, and experiment with his personal construction of his world, he needs to build a repertoire of skills which, like those of a research supervisor, will help this process along, and this inevitably implies a degree of expertise not available to his patients in the procedures of therapeutic 'research'. The therapist may use his ingenuity in what procedures he devises, though some are suggested by Kelly himself as likely to be of value in some cases at least. One such technique is 'fixed role therapy', in which the patient is invited to construct a role for himself which departs from his usual self-characterization in certain important respects. He is then asked to play this role in real life for a certain period of time (perhaps a week or two). This is, of course, to be seen as an experiment in which the patient exposes himself to new experiences which may enable him to reassess certain assumptions that he had about himself and his world, and not simply as an attempt to change people through play-acting. In order successfully to facilitate such experimentation, the therapist must, in Kelly's view as in Freud's, keep himself as a *person* resolutely in the background: if he is not exactly a Freudian 'screen for projections', he is something rather like it, and should be sure that he is 'interpretable by the client in a variety of ways'.[17] The difference between him and the psychoanalyst is that he may potentiate examination of these interpretations through the deliberate use of role-play; he may produce, that is, different personalities for different occasions, depending upon his judgment of the individual's experimental needs at the time.

This picture of the therapist operating, so to speak, 'within himself', consciously varying his self-presentation, together with the more general emphasis on role-playing in therapy, illustrates the important part played by consciously directed behaviour in Kelly's system. The central aim of therapy thus becomes one of increasing the person's *awareness* of what he is doing and how he is constructing his world. The ability to become aware of oneself and one's 'constructs', and hence to become more skilled in the elaboration of a complex and sensitive set of interpretations through which one's world can be ordered, is thus a fundamental value of personal construct psychotherapy. It is, however, important to recognize that self-conscious skills of this kind can only be used in a context, as a means to an end, and it is easy to slip into a view of them as ends in themselves. There can be no point in becoming more and more aware, more skilful in your construing of your world, if you are not increasing your skill and your awareness *for* something. Failure to recognize this—in any form of psychotherapy—leads to difficulties which will be discussed in a later chapter.

Most brands of psychotherapy which we have not so far considered—and there are still well over a hundred of them—rely for their credibility on focusing on one aspect or area of human psychology and making it central to their system. In this they are aided by the infinite variety of human concerns: whatever esoteric aspect of behaviour or motivation you annex for the basis of your very own patent therapy, there is bound to be someone to whom it makes sense and who will make a satisfactory disciple, if not a patient. The more important variants of psychotherapy, however, may gain impetus and influence by virtue of the fact that, though the same basic process is at work, the area of human psychology they highlight is one which has wide appeal and potential explanatory value, and yet has been so far neglected. Thus, though perhaps limited in terms of their general applicability, such therapies may combine novelty with insight in a way which promises considerable psychological utility. Though lightweight in relation to the monoliths of psychoanalysis and behaviourism, they are nevertheless forces to be reckoned with.

Berne's 'transactional analysis' provides an example of one such therapeutic school.[18] While there are some aspects of Berne's theory which seem to be little more than slightly modified and diluted psychoanalytic concepts, his central achievement was to bring to the attention of psychotherapists the importance of *interpersonal strategy* for an understanding of many of their patients' problems. (This was not, of course, a *discovery* of Berne's, but a view which he was particularly successful in articulating.) In essence, the kind of interpersonal strategies, or 'games', which Berne focused upon are those in which a person, through the covert manipulation of a social relationship, may arrive at a 'payoff' in which he extorts public acknowledgment of a role he is anxious to adopt. Martyrdom, for example, is particularly easy to achieve by means of suitable provocation, and, despite its necessary discomforts, offers rich rewards in terms of moral unassailability and self-righteousness. As with other modern variants of psychotherapy, transactional analysts emphasize the importance of the patient's *taking responsibility* for himself and his actions as part of the process of change.

'Rational-emotive psychotherapy', the creation of Albert Ellis,[19] seems to consist of an almost unbelievably eclectic set of techniques and theoretical justifications which Ellis nevertheless manages to organize around one or two more central ideas. In particular, he emphasizes the role played in neurotic behaviour by the inappropriate (irrational) standards and values the patient holds, and to which, consequently, he over-reacts emotionally. Thus Ellis's aim is to attack 'magical' personal philosophies with the weapons of 'logico-empiricism'. His somewhat optimistic theory is that 'emotional disturbance is little more than another name for devout religiosity, intolerance, whining, dogmatism, magical thinking and anti-scientism; and if people rigorously follow the logical-empirical approach and forego all forms of magic and absolutism it is virtually impossible for them to be seriously disturbed'.

Ellis's therapeutic technique is to confront the patient's irrational beliefs and values in the most direct manner possible, even hectoring or ridiculing him if this seems the only way in which he can be made to see reason. Thus the patient who feels that sexual rejection is a catastrophe of major proportions and is thereby led to despair and impotence, may be exposed to the full blast of Ellis's rational scorn as he is persuaded that such rejection, though unfortunate and frustrating perhaps, has nothing to say about him as a whole person. We are here a very long way indeed from the neutral, opaque psychoanalyst, or the concerned and yet non-directive Rogerian. Ellis represents instead the embodiment of a supremely confident view of man, certain of its aims and its ethics, and ready to proclaim its values by any means at its disposal which can remotely be considered rational. Such means vary from argument to behaviour-shaping of the Skinnerian variety, from ridicule to 'shame-attacking' assignments which require patients to behave foolishly or absurdly in order to demonstrate that doing so in fact results in no great catastrophe. In rational-emotive psychotherapy we again meet factors which are common to several of the recently developed psychotherapies: the belief, for example, that the patient gets *himself* into a situation which only he can get himself out of, and that effective or convincing personal experience will be arrived at, often, only through the patient's actually getting into certain situations and, so to speak, rehearsing them behaviourally. Self-awareness is less of an aim for Ellis than the banishment of self-delusion.

'Gestalt therapy', the parentage of which is again attributable to one man—Fritz Perls,[20] moves us further from the treatment of neurosis and more towards psychological 'growth'. Gestalt therapists are as concerned for the total well-being of the normal individual as they are with the cure of neurosis, and the therapeutic techniques they have devised are aimed at a number of areas of human functioning which are felt to be particularly important in the attainment of such well-being. Among these are a belief in the importance of bringing into awareness the *present* experience of the person as a *whole*. Thus not only what the person is thinking and feeling, but what he is doing with his body (how it feels to him, what he is expressing through it) *now*, in the present, will be the focus of therapeutic work. Again, there is a great deal of emphasis on the person's responsibility for himself, as well as upon the importance for him of self-acceptance, of allowing himself to become what he is. Much of the therapist's activity will thus consist of devising activities and experiences which will put the individual in the position of discovering what he is doing and intending in the immediately present therapeutic situation.

Gestalt therapy is perhaps the most influential of a wide variety of approaches which tend currently to be assembled under the headings 'humanistic psychology' or the 'growth movement'. These are too many and varied even to be enumerated here, and attack psychological problems from widely differing angles. There are the 'body therapies', for example, which attempt to relieve psychological blocks and tensions by concentrating upon and manipulating their supposed foci of emotional and nervous energy in the body, perhaps by means of various types of massage and movement; there are also the myriad kinds of 'encounter group', in which 'authentic' meeting between individuals is engineered by a wide range of techniques, from verbal confrontation to, literally, naked exposure to the gaze of others. The rationale of these approaches usually appeals to some variety of Western or Eastern thinking, or a combination of the two, which stresses the importance of immediate experience, authentic, genuine relationships, and freedom. They tend to share a contempt for the narrow objectivism of orthodox Western psychology and philosophy, but beyond this, identification of common theoretical strands is difficult. Certainly, many of these approaches betray a fierce moralism which makes no secret of its aims for mankind. As Rowan[21] states them: 'Self-understanding, greater autonomy, increased spontaneity and creativity, a higher ethical awareness, lowered defensiveness, clearer perception, greater ability to take risks.' One might be forgiven for thinking that such a programme marks a radical departure from the traditional scientism of behaviourism and psychoanalysis; that we have found at last a way out of the mechanism and determinism which is the hallmark of so much of psychology and psychotherapy.

And yet, curiously, this does not often seem to be the case, and the aspirations of humanistic psychology seem to reflect more a modification of the message than a change in the medium. There is, for example, a certain paradoxical quality about the work of Abraham Maslow,[22] one of the high priests of the humanistic camp. For, having noted that some individuals seem to have achieved higher planes of psychological 'being' and creativeness than others, he goes on to suggest that a study of their methods, so to speak, will enable the rest of us to reach the same peaks. This uncovers a kind of crude, mechanistic pragmatism which surely, in fact, makes nonsense of human achievement. Again, the lofty aspirations in terms of human goals one finds in humanistic psychological literature are sometimes found to mask a strangely contrasting materialism. This, for example, is betrayed in a remark of Maslow's which Rowan quotes in his book. Having gone some way towards identifying his ideal person, Maslow suggests that 'the society which can turn out such people will survive; the societies which *cannot* turn out such people will die.' One is almost left wondering why Maslow did not enlist the support of B. F. Skinner in 'turning out' such people by means of conditioning techniques.

Neither are we, in the growth movement, freed from the mystique of the experts and their superior vision of what is good for us: they are always ready, it seems, to tell us what is, as Rowan puts it, 'more healthy and truly human than the average'. Malcolm Brown, for example, in a paper on 'the new body psychotherapies',[23] informs us that: 'Any person who cannot acknowledge the importance, and directly listen to, the wisdom of his own body is psychologically crippled and neurotic.' A slightly longer quotation from this paper, in which Brown discusses Reichian therapy, will serve usefully to illustrate the extraordinary quality of mixed mysticism and mechanism which is often to be found in such approaches:

Reich discovered that the curtailment of the longitudinal life-energy flow went hand in hand with the active maintenance of the repressive forces of the ego-defences within the neurotic psyche, and that one very effective way to loosen these repressive forces was to directly attack the seven rings of muscular armouring which pervaded the tension-racked body of the neurotic. By systematically attacking each ring by various direct body-contact techniques the Reichian therapist discovered that the patient's ego-defence system could rapidly be blasted open from underneath.

Sigmund Koch, one of the most thoughtful observers of the psychological scene, states a view of this kind of approach in psychotherapy with which it is hard not to agree:

... the group movement is the most extreme excursion so far of man's talent for reducing, distorting, evading, and vulgarizing his own reality. It is also the most poignant exercise of that talent, for it seeks and promises to do the very reverse. It is adept at the image-making manoeuvre of evading human reality in the very process of seeking to discover and enhance it. It seeks to court spontaneity and authenticity by artifice; to combat instrumentalism instrumentally; to provide access to experience by reducing it to a packaged commodity; to engineer autonomy by group pressure; to liberate individuality by group shaping. Within the lexicon of its concepts and methods, openness becomes transparency; love, caring and sharing become a barter of 'reinforcements' or perhaps mutual ego-titillation; aesthetic receptivity or immediacy becomes 'sensory awareness'. It can provide only a grotesque simulacrum of every noble quality it courts. It provides, in effect, a convenient psychic whorehouse for the purchase of a gamut of well-advertised existential 'goodies': authenticity, freedom, wholeness, flexibility, community, love, joy. One enters for such liberating consummations but inevitably settles for psychic strip-tease.[24]

The sad thing is that, having identified, so it seems, some of the major ills of traditional approaches in psychology and psychotherapy, humanistic psychologists have lacked the intellectual discipline and moral sensitivity to provide a carefully worked-out alternative. While deploring the fruits of traditional psychology, they have not been sufficiently critical of its methods, and indeed have often mindlessly applied the same mechanistic and deterministic assumptions in pursuit of their own goals, without apparently becoming aware of the paradox involved in doing so. Thus the psychotherapist in search of a scientific formulation of what he is doing is likely to find in the humanistic psychologies either a disguised version of orthodox mechanism, etc., or a contemptuous dismissal of all intellectual discipline combined with an untrammelled moral fervour. The emphasis placed by humanistic psychotherapists on the significance of relationships, the importance of immediate experience to understanding and change, the responsibility of the individual, and so on, is undoubtedly valuable, and continues a tradition in modern psychotherapy which started with Jung. But the methods used to exploit these insights, and to reach towards the moral goals which seem so self-evident to the humanistic therapists, are too often simple-minded and artificial, and typify just that mechanistic use of technique to which one would expect their authors most to object. (I am thinking here, for example, of such things as the use of nudity as a token of psychological self-exposure; the ventilation of anger at somebody by hitting a pillow which represents him; the self-conscious use of embrace or eye-contact as a means of generating intimacy between strangers, and so on and on.)

Though theoreticians of psychotherapy of the stature of Rogers and Kelly have gone a long way towards issuing a fundamental challenge to the traditional psychotherapies, the implications of

what they have said for a change in the basic scientific structure of
psychotherapy do not seem to have been accepted and elaborated,
often even by their own followers, enough to lay the ghosts of
objectivist impersonality, mechanism and determinism in psychotherapy. And even the challengers themselves may not always have
seen where their insights were leading them to, or, if they did, may
have taken fright at the extent to which a rejection of traditional
scientific values in psychology would have to go. For if he is to
become personal, subjective, dynamic and indeterminist, to give up
the general for the particular, is there any sense at all in which the
therapist can still consider himself scientific? If you see science as a
method, the answer is probably 'no'. If, on the other hand, you see
science as a certain kind of *stance* towards your own observation and
experience, the answer may yet be 'yes'. My own view, already stated
earlier, is that scientific method originated as a means whereby
scientists could free their own experience from (largely religious)
dogma. That means has, in psychology, now itself become dogmatic,
and places a barrier between the psychologist and his subject-
matter, such that he can no longer take it *seriously*, but must distort
what he sees in order to maintain the relevance of his methodology.
Much of the rest of this book will constitute an attempt to suggest
what changes we shall have to make in our view of scientific method
if we are to regain a relationship of good faith with our *experience* as
psychologists. In other words, I hope to explore some of the
conclusions psychotherapists may have to draw about the nature of
psychotherapy if they are to take their experience with their patients
seriously.

For there is no doubt that, despite the inroads that psychotherapists have made into some of the more constricting
assumptions of orthodox psychoanalysis and behaviourism, the
dogmas of traditional science still haunt psychotherapy. But, to
return to a question I have already raised earlier, why does all this
matter? If, as is probably the case, psychotherapists have recognized
that what they do may benefit their patients no matter what they *say*
they do, why should we need to become so concerned with their
scientific theorizing and the implicit values it contains? Am I not
simply involved in attacking straw men and obtusely failing to
acknowledge the great pragmatic advances which therapists of all
kinds have made?

My answer is that these dogmatic scientific values, implicit and
deeply buried in the infrastructure of psychotherapy as they often
are, can, and sometimes do, wreak havoc in what we actually do to

patients. I shall illustrate this answer with a cautionary tale.

In a paper entitled 'Septal Stimulation of the Initiation of Hetero-sexual Behavior in a Homosexual Male', Moan and Heath report a form of behavioural treatment for homosexuality which was published in the *Journal of Behaviour Therapy and Experimental Psychiatry* in 1972, and reprinted in *Psychotherapy and Behavior Change 1972*, an annual publication of the Aldine Publishing Company, Chicago, whose editors evidently thought the paper sufficiently important for inclusion among 'the most significant literature published in the field of psychotherapy' for that year.

'Patient B-19', as the authors named him, was a young man with a long record of disturbed behaviour, drug abuse and homosexual activity. Among many other things, the authors describe him as 'hypersensitive to criticism and unreasonably self-conscious in public', 'disdainful, arrogant and grandiose', demonstrating paranoia 'often of true psychotic proportions', 'a severe procrastinator', depressed and preoccupied with suicidal ideas. He was also diagnosed as suffering from temporal lobe epilepsy. The authors' aim was to change B-19's homosexual behaviour by reinforcing (rewarding) heterosexual responses—a procedure they took to be reasonable on the grounds of 'the large number of studies reporting the effectiveness of various operational forms of pleasure in altering or "counterconditioning" undesired human behaviors'. The reinforcing stimulus was achieved by implanting electrodes into the septal region of the patient's brain; a number of electrodes were planted into other brain areas at the same time. Electrical stimulation of the electrodes in the septal region brought about subjectively pleasurable sensations for B-19.

Suitably wired up in this way, B-19 was next snown 'a 15-min. 8mm "stag" film featuring sexual intercourse and related activities between a male and a female'—an experience he did not appear to enjoy. Following this, he was introduced to septal stimulation, controlled both by the experimenters and himself. 'He likened these responses to the pleasurable states he had sought and experienced through the use of amphetamines', and indeed during self-stimulation sessions 'B-19 stimulated himself to a point that, both behaviourally and introspectively, he was experiencing an almost overwhelming euphoria and elation and had to be disconnected, despite his vigorous protests'. Following this experience B-19 showed a 'notable improvement in disposition and behaviour, was less recalcitrant and more co-operative . . . and reported increasing interest in female personnel and feelings of arousal with a compulsion to masturbate'. On being shown the stag film for a second time, discreetly watched through one-way glass by the experimenters, he became sexually aroused during the performance, 'had an erection, and masturbated to orgasm'. For the next few days the patient showed increased interest in women and preoccupation with sex. In view of the success of the programme so far, the therapist/experimenters moved on to the next phase of the treatment, which was to introduce B-19 to 'a 21-year-old prostitute' for a two-hour encounter (carefully described by the authors) in a specially prepared laboratory, towards the end of which time he was able to reach orgasm in sexual intercourse 'despite the milieu and the encumbrance of the electrode wires', which latter enabled the experimenters to make physiological recordings of the proceedings.

The outcome of this treatment is viewed favourably by the authors, despite the fact that B-19, 'while he looks and is apparently functioning better . . . still has a complaining disposition which does not permit him readily to admit his progress'. He subsequently had a ten-month sexual relationship with a married woman, whereas, they report, 'homosexual behaviour has occurred only twice, when he needed money and "hustling" was a quick way to get it when he was out of work'. The authors feel that 'the success reported points toward future effective use of septal activation for reinforcing desired behavior and extinguishing undesired behavior', and they comment that 'plans for such treatment programs are under way . . . and will be activated in the near future'.

The reader will, I hope, be able to draw his own conclusions from this rather bizarre story, and will be able to relate the account of it to the discussion preceding it. What is quite plain is that a passion for objectivity and impersonality, leading, for example, to the pointless use of the designation 'B-19' and the provision of details of the gauge and duration of the pornographic film, the age of the prostitute, etc., results in an almost total blindness to the human significance of the procedures used. We are not told, for example, why this patient's general homosexuality was considered 'undesirable' when, by contrast, homosexual 'hustling' for money is passed over as more or less all right. There is no discussion in the paper of how the experiment (which necessitated a potentially dangerous brain operation) was presented and justified to the patient, and indeed his apparent feeling that it had not done him much good is dismissed as characteristic of a 'complaining disposition'. Again, his former drug abuse is mentioned disapprovingly in his history as evidence, presumably, of more 'undesirable behaviour', and yet part of the cure consists in providing him with a direct means of stimulating his brain, which in fact reminds him most of the joys of amphetamine. We are, in other words, lost in a technological fairyland (or nightmare), the mechanistic and impersonal values of which are taken as self-evidently valid, and in which the individual's subjective experience is overlooked as of no consequence. The occupants of this technological world, since it precludes consideration of such things, have only an astoundingly crude and rudimentary understanding of human experience and ethics, and hence no possibility of being self-critical in these respects. It is no surprise, therefore, that they can unblushingly betray the extraordinary poverty of their own values, themselves totally untouched by any kind of rational scrutiny, in speaking of 'undesirable' or 'desirable' behaviour, or in preferring their own judgment of whether a patient 'looks better' to what he himself resists 'admitting'. What we are dealing with, it seems to me, is not science, but a set of dogmatic principles which shows signs of running riot and crushing our capacity to think. The above example may be extreme, but it is not atypical of a significant proportion of what passes for psychotherapy.

We already have, then, some hints of what an alternative scientific philosophy for psychotherapy must be: in contrast to the present dogmatic orthodoxy it must take account of the personal, the subjective, the dynamic and the non-deterministic. Before we explore whether such a scientific philosophy is possible, and how it might change the appearance of psychotherapy, we should perhaps look to the research literature on psychotherapy to see what lessons it may have to offer us. This will be the task of the following chapter.

1 For the current spectrum in psychotherapy see D. Bannister (ed.). (1975). *Issues and Approaches in the Psychological Therapies.* New York and London: Wiley. For an historical perspective see D. Wyss. (1966). *Depth Psychology: a Critical History.* London: Allen & Unwin.

2 A satisfactory initial source is J. A. C. Brown. (1964). *Freud and the Post-Freudians.* Harmondsworth: Penguin Books. The writings of Freud himself are by no means as impenetrable as the non-professional reader might suspect. The *Introductory Lectures to Psychoanalysis* and the *New Introductory Lectures to Psychoanalysis,* and *The Interpretation of Dreams*—perhaps Freud's major work—are titles available in a number of editions.

3 Freud, S. (1933). Femininity. In *New Introductory Lectures on Psycho-Analysis.* Published by W. W. Norton, Inc., 1965 (p. 132) and in Penguin Books, 1973. *Standard Edition of the Complete Works of Sigmund*

   Freud (1915). Trans. and ed. James Strachey. Vol. XXII. London: the
   Hogarth Press.
 4 A readable initial source is V. Meyer and E. Chesser. (1970). *Behaviour
   Therapy in Clinical Psychiatry.* Harmondsworth: Penguin Books.
 5 Criticisms of behaviourism in general psychology have been made by
   S. Koch. (1964). Psychology and emerging conceptions of knowledge as
   unitary. In T. W. Wann (ed.) *Behaviorism and Phenomenology.*
   Chicago: Univ. Chicago Press. For a more recent work embodying
   similar criticism see R. Poole. (1972). *Towards Deep Subjectivity.*
   Harmondsworth: Allen Lane, The Penguin Press. In the field of
   psychotherapy particularly cogent criticisms have been put by L. Breger
   and J. L. McGaugh. (1965). Critique and reformulation of 'learning
   theory' approaches to psychotherapy and neurosis. *Psychological
   Bulletin.* **63**, 338.
 6 Cliffe, M. J., Gathercole, C. and Epling, W. F. (1974). Some implications
   of the experimental analysis of behaviour for behaviour modification.
   Bulletin of the British Psychological Society, **27**, 390.
 7 Jung, C. G. (1954). *The Practice of Psychotherapy.* Collected Works,
   Vol. XVI, p. 71. London: Routledge & Kegan Paul.
 8 ibid.
 9 Guntrip, H. (1971). The ego psychology of Freud and Adler re-examined
   in the 1970s. *British Journal of Medical Psychology*, **44**, 305.
10 Lazarus, A. (1971). *Behavior Therapy and Beyond.* New York: McGraw
   Hill.
11 A good account can be found in C. Rogers. (1961). *On Becoming a
   Person.* London: Constable.
12 Rogers, C. R. (1957). The necessary and sufficient conditions of
   therapeutic personality change. *Journal of Consulting Psychology*, **21**,
   95.
13 Rogers, C. R. (1964). Toward a science of the person. In T. W. Wann
   (ed.) *Behaviorism and Phenomenology.* Chicago: Univ. Chicago Press.
14 Wexler, D. A. and Rice, L. N. (1974). *Innovations in Client-Centred
   Therapy.* New York: Wiley.
15 See the chapters by Ludwig Binswanger in R. May (ed.). (1958).
   Existence. New York: Basic Books.
16 Kelly, G. A. (1955). *The Psychology of Personal Constructs.* Vols. I and
   II. New York: Norton. See also D. Bannister and F. Fransella. (1971).
   Inquiring Man. Harmondsworth: Penguin Books.
17 Kelly, G. A. op. cit., Vol. II, p. 620.
18 For an entertaining introduction to 'transactional analysis' see E. Berne.
   (1964). *Games People Play.* New York: Grove Press.
19 See, for example, A. Ellis (1975). Rational-emotive psychotherapy. In
   D. Bannister (ed.) *Issues and Approaches in the Psychological
   Therapies.* London and New York: Wiley.
20 Perls, F. S. (1969). *Gestalt Therapy Verbatim.* Lafayette: Real People
   Press.

21 Rowan, J. (1976). *Ordinary Ecstasy. Humanistic Psychology in Action.* London: Routledge & Kegan Paul.
22 Maslow, A. H. (1962). *Toward a Psychology of Being.* Princeton: Van Nostrand.
23 Brown, M. (1973). The new body psychotherapies. *Psychotherapy: Theory, Research and Practice,* **10**, 98.
24 Koch, S. (1971). The image of man implicit in encounter group theory. *Journal of Humanistic Psychology,* **11**, 109.

3

Research in Psychotherapy

It is unfortunately not possible simply to detail research findings in psychotherapy as if they were established 'scientific facts'. This is so, if for no other reason, because such 'facts' as there are more often than not tend to contradict one another, and also because research in psychotherapy is not carried out by disinterested, 'objective' automata, but by psychologists and psychotherapists who have a stake, not only in what they 'discover', but also in where they start looking. If, for example, your primary interest is to ascertain the degree to which your clients reach a higher state of 'being', your research strategies are likely to be very different from those you would adopt if your only aim is to rid patients of the neurotic 'symptoms' they complain of at their initial interview. Pyscho-therapists, in other words, have widely differing values, and these determine the context of their research.

In recent years there has been an explosion in research into psychotherapy which has resulted in a very extensive literature, a thorough review of which would not be feasible for this book. I shall therefore limit myself to a discussion of some of the problems which face the research worker in this area, together with an examination of some of the research results which are most germane to the central preoccupations of this work. Extensive reviews of the psychotherapy research literature are available elsewhere.[1]

For many years—most of the first half of this century—research publications on the nature and effectiveness of psychotherapy consisted for the most part of individual case reports written by practitioners of the more or less orthodox psychoanalytic school and its derivatives. A typical paper of this kind would thus consist of a description of the patient and a formulation of his problems, together with an account of the course of treatment and an assessment of the outcome. Quite clearly such reports must be selective in the sense that the analyst's view of what are the important events in therapy will be determined by what he is looking for, and by the theoretical framework in which he places his activity.

45

For this reason, case histories of the kind we are considering are not (indeed, *could* not be) purely objective descriptions of what happened between the analyst and his patient during the course of therapy and what befell the patient as the result (such a description would involve an infinity of observations, most of them trivial and boring in the extreme); rather, they assume the validity of a particular theoretical standpoint, and describe the events of therapy in the terms allowed by that standpoint. In this way, a psychoanalytic case report would take for granted the validity of psychoanalytic thinking in some important and central respects— they might focus, for example, on the 'Oedipal conflict' evident in the 'transference relationship', feeling it unnecessary, in view of the work already carried out by Freud and others, to pause in their account in order to justify the use of such concepts.

The model on which this kind of research was based is obviously a medical one, and makes the same kind of assumptions that would be made, for example, in a report of the treatment of a case of tuberculosis. It assumes that a diagnosis (or formulation) has been made which is reliably similar to diagnoses which can be made in a significant number of other cases; it assumes that an established treatment procedure has been carried out which could be reliably replicated by others, and which bears upon (in this case psychological) structures which the patient shares with others to an identifiable extent. It further assumes that the technical language used and the experiences described are shared by other professional workers to an extent sufficient to make their communication worth-while. Now all these assumptions, and others like them, may be justifiable in an account of the treatment of tuberculosis (though this, as we shall see, is debatable), but even a cursory exploration of the psychotherapy literature suggests that their justifiability does not extend to the psychological sphere. There are two sets of reasons for this, one of which I shall call radical, and the other non-radical. I shall deal first with the non-radical objections to the individual case report kind of research which we have so far discussed, since these are the ones which specifically apply to it. Radical objections apply both to the case study research and to the research methodology which has largely replaced it, and I shall consider these a little later on.

The main point of non-radical objections to the psychoanalytic case study approach is simply that it is not succeeding in what it sets out to do—not (which is the radical objection) that its aims are misconceived in the first place. Thus the non-radical critic will accept that the proper aim of research into psychotherapy is to arrive at findings which are generalizable to certain (possibly diagnostic) groups of patients in terms of the treatment techniques which must be applied to bring about amelioration or cure; he will not accept, however, that the proper approach to such generalizable findings is through the study and report of individual cases. His objections, furthermore, will have more or less equal application in physical as well as psychological disorder, and centre on the lack of objectivity inevitably involved in the case study approach.

The psychoanalyst, it might be argued, has an emotional stake in what he is doing, and hence may be biased in his perception of a patient's improvement. His view of what happens, therefore, needs to be backed up by objective measurement. The theoretical assumptions he makes have themselves not been objectively validated, and may (indeed, fairly obviously do) vary from those of his colleagues, so that different therapists only *appear* to be talking about the same things. The diagnostic criteria he uses may well be largely personal, unless the contrary can be objectively demonstrated, and so his results will not be comparable with those of others. He has no way of knowing whether what happens to his patient is the result of his intervention, or is due to other factors entirely; this could only be established through the use of a proper experimental methodology which makes use, for example, of matched groups of patients in which a treated group is compared with an untreated control group according to measurable criteria. The therapist who relies on anecdotal accounts of what happens to individual patients in psychotherapy for the advancement of his knowledge has, in short, missed the scientific boat. To save himself, he must adopt more rigorously objective methods and submit his procedures to far more searching experimental scrutiny.

The type of research methodology relevant to these non-radical criticisms is in principle readily to hand in experimental psychology, which has long been concerned with just these kinds of problems. And it is to behavioural scientists trained in the academic discipline of psychology that we largely owe the bulk of research findings, such as they are, in psychotherapy. Many of these people are, it is true, clinical psychologists engaged in the practice of psychotherapy; nevertheless, they owe a scientific allegiance to their parent discipline, and it is this which determines their approach to research. Before turning to some of the broader and more radical criticisms which can be made of psychotherapeutic research strategies as a whole, we should consider what the experimentally more rigorous and objective approaches have unearthed.

In a now famous (or notorious, depending on your perspective) paper in the early 1950s, H. J. Eysenck[2] launched an attack on psychotherapy which was probably in large part responsible for the explosion in research work in this area which followed. Critical of the subjective nature of most reports upholding the effectiveness of psychotherapy, Eysenck showed that a consideration of such objective research studies as there were suggested no evidence in favour of a positive outcome, and indeed it seemed that psychotherapy could not be assumed to show any more beneficial effect than no treatment at all. Eysenck, whose preference is for treatment methods based on behaviourist approaches to learning theory, tended to use his findings as a basis for rejecting psychotherapy altogether as a valid undertaking (and by 'psychotherapy' he mainly meant broadly psychoanalytic methods). Other research workers,[3] however, were quick to point out that even from the objectivist point of view that Eysenck himself adopted, this conclusion is not justified by his observations. While it was clear that, taking 'psychotherapy' as a broadly uniform procedure, and assuming comparability of patients across rather diverse research studies, psychotherapy could not be shown to 'work' better than no treatment at all, to *make* these assumptions of uniformity and comparability itself involved an inadequate degree of objectivity and experimental rigour. What was needed, so it was argued, was to make a much finer differentiation between the kinds of techniques used, the kinds of therapists practising them and the kinds of patients they applied them to. One could not simply take, for example, 'psychoanalysts' and see if their 'neurotic patients' 'improved' more than patients who had merely been kept on a waiting list. The reasons why this cannot be done are obvious: psychoanalysts vary amongst themselves both personally and in terms of the techniques they use; patients differ from each other, and diagnosis is more an art than a science; 'improving' involves a wide range of criteria which will vary from therapist to therapist and research study to research study—some might focus on the subjective feelings of the patients, others on a more objective criterion such as vocational, social or sexual adequacy.

It thus came to be recognized that any research study in this area should focus *at least* on the following: the personal as well as the technical and theoretical differences between therapists; the personal as well as the diagnostic differences between patients; differences in criteria for successful outcome; differences in the environmental circumstances of patients during treatment, and so on.

The initial flood of research reports claiming greater objectivity than the psychoanalytic case report approach came largely from the behaviour therapy camp. Flushed with what they saw as the success of Eysenck's damnation of conventional psychotherapy, it was not long before behaviour therapists were publishing strikingly dramatic claims for the success of their methods. Wolpe, for example, claimed a success rate of 90 per cent in the treatment by systematic desensitization of anxiety neurotics.[4] However, it soon became apparent that many of these claims were based less on the sober use of a thoroughly objective research methodology than on a kind of scientific virtue-by-association, as it were, with the behaviourist philosophy underlying the treatment methods, and it was not long before such claims were modified. At the same time, more and more voices were being raised in criticism of a crude 'outcome' approach to research in psychotherapy, and a proper respect for the kinds of problems mentioned in the last paragraph began to develop.

The unfolding of research strategies and findings cannot be traced in detail here, but it may be of interest to consider some of the most salient features to emerge.

What seems particularly evident is that, as I suggested at the beginning of Chapter 2, what therapists *say* they do in psychotherapy is less relevant, in terms of what actually happens, than what they *do* do (this, however, is most emphatically *not* to say that what they say they do is unimportant in a general sense, as I hope I have shown in the previous chapter). A number of studies, for example, suggest that experienced therapists of *different* theoretical persuasions are more likely to behave similarly in their relations with their patients than are inexperienced compared to experienced therapists of the *same* theoretical school.[5] Much of the work in this area was carried out in response to the criticisms and claims of the behaviour therapists, who can be seen (from the perspective of the non-radical critic) to have goaded their more 'mentalistic' colleagues into a more responsible research attitude. Again, however much therapists may focus on the *technical* aspects of their procedures, an increasing body of evidence suggests that it is the *personal* relationship between themselves and their patients which is experienced by the latter as the most potent therapeutic force. Whitehorn and Betz carried out a pioneering study in this area[6] which showed that therapists of a particular personality type were more successful in the treatment of schizophrenics than therapists of a contrasting personality type. Research workers in the Rogerian camp similarly demonstrated in some detail[7] that therapists who offered the therapeutic 'conditions' of warmth, empathy and genuineness tended to be more successful in Rogers' client-centred therapy than those who did not—the latter, indeed, could be positively harmful to their clients. Even some psychotherapists of the more orthodox psychoanalytic variety found in their research[8] that technical procedures seemed relatively less important than personal factors. Such findings have been reinforced, if only indirectly, by further research evidence[9] that the very orientation a professional therapist adopts is likely to be determined as much by factors related to his personal characteristics and social attitudes as by any cool scientific assessment of its validity.

In this way, some of the more obviously constricting mechanistic assumptions underlying psychotherapy have been subjected to great strain—indeed, can be said to have been cracked—by empirical scrutiny. Not, of course, that the debate has been carried on without rancour. Whatever may be the case in the natural sciences (and it may not be so different), psychological research certainly does not proceed in a uniformly disinterested spirit of scientific inquiry: almost any research study can be questioned on methodological grounds, and alternative hypotheses for its findings can be advanced. Because of this, few psychoanalysts will have abandoned their theoretical beliefs on the evidence mentioned above, nor will many behaviour therapists feel that the aseptic rigour of their scientific dogma will not emerge triumphant in the end. There is little doubt, however, that the fervour of both sides has been modified by such findings, as is witnessed by the somewhat more temperate language in which they tend these days to express their views in the scientific literature.

The personal qualities of patients have perhaps received rather less attention in the research literature than those of their therapists. This relative lack of attention may perhaps reflect the passive position which patients still tend to occupy in the therapeutic equation. The therapist is active, and hence his personal contribution is likely to come into focus; the patient is to be acted upon, and hence his personal features are likely to be rather less salient. Even so, most research studies make some effort at describing patients in greater detail than would be afforded by the bare allocation of a diagnosis. Most psychotherapists are probably agreed in rejecting the inappropriate medical framework implied by purely diagnostic preoccupations, and will tend to look at their patients in terms of objective descriptions of their sex, age and socio-economic status, as well as a more or less factual description of the kinds of problems and behaviours they present. In this way such terms as 'anxious', 'phobic', 'obsessional', etc., may be used more as broad descriptions of behaviour than as imputations of distinct types of illness.

Looking at patients in these respects has in a number of studies revealed a trend which is frequently noted by research workers with some concern, if not alarm, and that is that the kind of patient to enter psychotherapy with the best chance of success can be loosely characterized as (relatively) young, attractive, verbal, intelligent and successful. This leads many therapists to feel that their best efforts are spent upon those who least need them. There seems to be little agreement among research workers as to why such patients should do better than others, though these findings lead to the speculation that psychotherapies tend to be middle-class undertakings with middle-class values, and hence are likely to appeal most to those who are most like their originators and practitioners. There are indeed suggestions in the research literature that psychotherapy is most effective where values are shared between therapist and patient, but the business of matching one to the other on these grounds has not been taken far as yet. It does however seem possible that, just as the therapist may choose his orientation on the basis of what he finds appealing to his personal values and characteristics, so the patient may, so to speak, choose his 'symptoms' in accordance with his personal stance towards the world. In this respect a number of studies suggest[10] that whether or not a patient experiences his problems as primarily psychological distress on the one hand or somatic discomfort on the other may depend upon a more generally 'psychological' or 'objective' personal orientation to the world. The implications this might have for matching patient to treatment may well prove to be a central feature of future orthodox research in psychotherapy.[11]

In general, the findings of research workers in the field of psychotherapy tend not to provide the kind of answers which one might naïvely have hoped they would. It is not possible, for example, to say whether Freudian psychoanalysis works better than Jungian analytical psychology, whether encounter groups are better than individual psychotherapy, whether systematic desensitization is more effective than interpretations of the transference (see page 17). Not that studies have not been carried out to attempt such answers: they have simply failed to produce any consistent picture, in part at

least because of the enormous complexity of the psychotherapeutic
situation. What we have instead is a number of suggestions that
what looked to be important in psychotherapy—the technique
adopted, the orientation of the therapist—is in fact less important
than the operation of factors, such as the personal qualities of the
therapist, previously thought by many psychotherapists to be of no
account.

In fact there is no indication that any one kind of therapeutic
approach is overwhelmingly more beneficial than any other. All
approaches, from the psychoanalytic to the behavioural, tend to
result in an improvement of about two-thirds of the clientèle and a
lack of improvement in about one-third. This is, of course, about the
average for a great many studies, using widely different methods of
assessing improvement; while individual studies may differ
significantly from the two-thirds/one-third ratio, there is no overall
trend to support any particular technique or orientation against
others.

Perhaps this finding, as well as some of the other points that have
been made, could best be illustrated by referring in a little more
detail to one of the most recent, and in many ways one of the most
adequate (of its kind) research studies to have been carried out.

The study in question was carried out by R. B. Sloane and
colleagues, and subsequently published as a book.[12] The central
comparison made was between analytically oriented and
behaviourally oriented therapists in terms of the effectiveness of
their treatments with a group of patients typical of those requesting
help at an outpatient clinic. The research was well designed in a
number of respects: the therapists were experienced and respected
representatives of their orientation; the patients were also genuinely
representative of their group (many research studies rely on only
mildly disturbed undergraduate volunteers for their subjects); the
treated groups were compared to an untreated, waiting-list group;
judgments of improvement were made from ratings given by
psychiatrists who were not themselves involved in treating the
patients; a number of objective measurements of symptoms and
personality were made, as were measurements of the personal style
of the therapists; patients were followed up over a period of two
years. In short, the investigators took into account very nearly all the
factors which previous research had suggested may be of importance
to therapeutic effectiveness.

A thorough analysis by the investigators of the influence of all
these measured factors on therapeutic outcome revealed only

relatively minor differences between the two types of treatment. In fact, both kinds of therapy proved effective, and indeed more effective than previous research has often suggested. About 90 per cent of the total group of patients improved in respect of the main symptoms of which they originally complained, 75 per cent improved in their social adjustment, and 70 per cent in their work adjustment. There were measurable differences between therapists in terms of the style of their work—how 'directive' they were, etc.—but these proved to have little effect on the overall outcome. Measurement of the personal qualities of therapists thought by Rogers and his associates to be important (warmth, empathy and genuineness) also failed to show significant effects on final outcome. In this respect, however, it is of interest to note that patients who *perceived* their therapists to be warm and genuine (irrespective, that is, of how warm and genuine they could be *measured* to be objectively) improved more than patients who saw these qualities as less characteristic of their therapists.

Thus, neither the technical approach of the therapists nor their personal characteristics as measured objectively showed any signs of making much difference to the degree of improvement of the patients, who, however, did improve significantly more than the untreated group. This kind of finding does, of course, leave the mechanistic psychologist in rather a quandary, hopeful though it is in many respects for the future of psychotherapy. His problem is that he still does not know what it is about psychotherapy that is effective. His natural reaction is that it must be some kind of 'non-specific' component of the therapeutic situation which he has so far failed to identify, something encompassed neither by the technical operations of the therapist nor by enduring and measurable features of his personality, but nevertheless something that diligent search cannot fail in the end to unearth.

The research workers in this case did not fail to ask the patients themselves what they found to be helpful in their treatment, though, not surprisingly (in view of their orthodox scientific scruples), they are somewhat reluctant to take the answers seriously. Nevertheless, the answers they did get, 'subjective' though they may be, are interesting. At least 70 per cent of the successfully treated patients, regardless of whether their treatment was analytic or behavioural, rated the following items as extremely, or very important: (1) the personality of your doctor; (2) his helping you to understand your problems; (3) encouraging you gradually to practise facing the things that bother you; (4) being able to talk to an understanding person;

(5) helping you to understand yourself. Patients who did well in analytically oriented therapy also felt the following items to be important: (1) encouraging you to shoulder your own responsibilities by restoring confidence in yourself; (2) the skill of your therapist; (3) his confidence that you will improve.

It is inevitable that issues such as these—issues of relationship, understanding, encouragement, responsibility, and so on—should be treated with caution by conventional behavioural scientists (and there is no doubt that Sloane *et al* treat them cautiously). They certainly do not fit snugly into the orthodox categories of psychology and psychotherapy, challenging as they do any conception of psychotherapy as a procedure whereby the expert therapist 'changes' the passive patient. These are issues which must, if they are to be taken seriously, be translated into a language which takes due account of the necessary rigours of mechanism and determinism, and which consequently enables them to be identified objectively and measurably as 'variables' in the behavioural equation. Only after such identification could they be manipulated precisely enough to be of consistent benefit to patients. Whether or not such a translation should be undertaken, furthermore, must depend upon the reliance which can be placed on what patients think to have been important in their treatment. What is important, from the standpoint of conventional psychology, is what has objectively taken place; what the patient *thinks* has taken place is, relatively speaking, neither here nor there.

Not all commentators on the psychotherapeutic scene, by any means, have failed to face the more obvious implications of the findings of this kind of research, even though they might not have seen just how far-reaching they could be. In what can perhaps best be described as an extremely sensible book on psychotherapy,[13] Jerome Frank considers therapeutic methods as just some among many approaches to *persuasion*. What these approaches have in common, he feels, are precisely those 'non-specific' factors which such studies as that of Sloane *et al* tend to reveal. Some of these factors Frank identifies as, for example, the trust the patient has in his therapist, his expectation of positive results, his emotional commitment to the therapeutic process, the stamp of social approval which therapeutic procedures carry, the fact that therapy makes certain demands on patients that they change themselves by active response to therapeutic directions, and so on. He also takes (as indeed do several other theorists of psychotherapy) a *relational* view of neurotic symptomatology: the patient uses his symptoms, in a manner which he conceals from himself, to control the behaviour of the 'significant others' around him. 'The aim of therapy then becomes', says Frank, 'to support the patient until he gets the courage to face what he is up to. This may then enable him to modify his goals in a healthier direction or change his behaviour in such a way that he gains them more effectively.' In a nutshell, Frank believes that: 'Psychotherapeutic procedures can be viewed as forms of personal influence that aim to provide the patient with morale-enhancing experiences that enable him to shed maladaptive patterns and adopt more successful ones.'

Frank's view of neurosis as a strategy for attempting to control others while evading the *responsibility* for so doing, his conceptualization of the process of therapy as one in which the patient gains the *courage* to alter his behaviour, and his assertion of the therapist's role as one of *personal influence*, are, I would feel, likely to evoke a sympathetic response in most psychotherapists who take their experience seriously. These, certainly, are some of the factors which seem to me most central, and they have the added merit of according closely with what patients themselves seem to feel to be of importance in their therapeutic experience. In view of this, it is curious that Frank does not, as far as I can see, draw the obvious conclusion: that a thoroughgoing science of psychotherapy must take these 'non-specific' factors as absolutely central to its field of inquiry. It must, that is, make them 'specific'. The reason why Frank does not draw this conclusion is presumably because, like so many others in this field, he is hamstrung by his conception of what it is to be 'scientific'. In the context of mechanism, determinism and objectivism, it is simply not possible to provide an adequate treatment of such factors as courage, responsibility and personal influence (impersonal influence would be all right). The result, for Frank, is that he is left with psychotherapy as one of the 'healing arts' of medicine, unable to fit it into a truly scientific framework until, for example, neurotic symptomatology has yielded an increased understanding of its biological bases. How, on his own account of such symptomatology, it could do this, remains an enigma. Nowhere in his book does Frank's consideration of the research findings in psychotherapy lead to a critical evaluation of the research methods themselves, nor does he question the relevance of the assumptions they make. Conventional research methodology aims at identifying the precise, 'specific' factors which can be shown to be operating mechanically and determinately in psychotherapy. The fact that it has failed to do so does not lead to a re-examination of the expectation that they *can* be identified, but to a vague dissatisfaction with psychotherapy as a scientifically understandable undertaking. Nor does a consideration of what findings there are in such research lead to the formulation of a theory that would account for them.

These observations lead us into what I called earlier a radical criticism of research methodology in the field of psychotherapy. The reason why psychotherapeutic writers and research workers are reluctant to undertake such a radical critique is because it is likely to change our conception of what it is to be scientific in this field. To many, the idea that this conception *can* be changed may appear merely ludicrous; to others it may seem to be a course that should be adopted only in the gravest extremity. In my judgment, that extreme has been reached. But before moving on to a consideration of what such an altered conception of science might look like, I should first indicate what my radical criticisms of psychotherapeutic research methodology are. They are not, I hasten to add, startlingly new or original. I merely wish them to be taken seriously.

Both the main orthodox approaches to research into psychotherapy—the individual case study as well as the group comparison approaches—make certain assumptions which, if they did not make them, would make nonsense of their own activity in the first place. It may be enough for our purpose to consider only three of these assumptions: (1) that the findings of research are generalizable; (2) that the subjects of research are static; (3) that the relation between researcher and researched is non-reflexive (i.e. the subjects of research must be manipulable by the research worker, but the latter must be immune to a similar kind of influence from the former).

It seems clear that if what you find to be the case with one patient could not be assumed to be the case with similar patients in similar circumstances, if what you find to be the case with a patient today is no longer found to be the case tomorrow, and if what you find to be the case with a patient leads him to *change* what is the case with him, then there seems very little point to your research enterprise in the first place. And yet precisely these are the problems which face all research workers in this area. So far, most of them have dealt with the problems by shutting their eyes tight and carrying on as before.

The central problem, of course, is that psychotherapy does not involve one set of rational, intelligent creatures dealing with another set of inanimate objects, but does involve one set of people dealing with another set of people who are in turn having to deal with the first set! Furthermore, people deal in *meanings* as well as purely physical, determinate events. Thus the significance of what a therapist does to a patient will depend, at least in part, upon the way the patient *interprets* what he does. And patients interpret things differently. To complicate matters further, the therapist will himself interpret the patient's interpretation, which may (or may not) lead him to modify his original action, and so on. To treat this kind of process, for research purposes, as if it were an operation in physics or chemistry is simply absurd. What happens to one person in psychotherapy cannot be generalized (except with the greatest caution) to others, because one person's psychotherapy involves a unique combination of two people's sets of meanings (his own and his therapist's). Patients do not remain static and psychologically inert while therapists tinker with their 'behaviour': they manoeuvre in response to their therapists' manoeuvres, and two different patients will respond to the same therapeutic manoeuvre differently. There is no way that the difficulties presented by this kind of situation can be reduced to the structural simplicity required by conventional research methodology. Don Bannister puts the problem well:[14]

The master chemist has finally produced a bubbling green slime in his test-tube, the potential of which is great but the properties of which are mysterious. He sits alone in his laboratory, test-tube in hand, brooding about what to do with the bubbling green slime. Then it slowly dawns on him that the bubbling green slime is sitting alone in the test-tube brooding about what to do with him. This special nightmare of the chemist is the permanent work-a-day world of the psychologist—the bubbling green slime is always wondering what to do about you.

The individual case report approach to research at least has the merit that some detailed consideration is given to the patient's individuality and special circumstances; but the view given is almost inevitably the view of one person (the writer of the report) who assumes that he is describing something 'objective', without taking into account the perspective which he describes it from, and assumes, wrongly, that another person in a similar 'objective' situation will reach similar conclusions. This is not to say that individual case reports are not *interesting*—they can be extremely illuminating in showing the *kind* of things which can happen in psychotherapy. What they cannot do is establish a particular procedure as correct for others; they cannot, that is, show people what to do in psychotherapy.

The group comparison approach to research, despite, or perhaps because of, the greater sophistication of its methodology of experimental design, is the more simplistic in terms of the assumptions made about people. People, that is, become exchangeable units, passively reacting to the various sorts of stimuli manipulated by the experimenter. In so far as your interest in people is precisely *as* exchangeable units (e.g. as election fodder, or consumers of instant coffee), this approach to research may have its uses, but as a potential method of clarifying what goes on in psychotherapy it is a disaster. This assumption of 'exchangeability' has led in the past to some glaringly silly research efforts, in which it was felt, for example, that a therapy for neurosis could be tested on students with fears of public speaking rather than genuine patients, or, again, in which therapists of one persuasion are trained in the techniques of another so that results of the two 'different' approaches can be compared.

But even in the absence of such crude mistakes as these, the methodological assumptions of such research mean that it can only be interested in the mechanical operation of certain invariant features of the therapeutic situation—ideally the techniques of the therapist, but if all else fails some invariant feature of his personality would do. This means that even if some insight *is* gained into the therapeutic process, it is quickly trivialized and rendered self-contradictory. The 'genuineness' of therapists is a good example: because this form of research must assume that 'genuineness' is an invariant quality that therapists do or do not 'have', research workers will, having discovered 'it' (in the first instance from what patients tell them), then set about training therapists to have it. Just to be sure of when its there and when it's not, they will then devise methods of measuring objectively the invariant property of genuineness they have (like ZX 14 in toothpaste) now isolated. In reality, of course, we then have a group of therapists trained in ingenuine genuineness (which nevertheless must be 'real' because it's measurable), but who, lo and behold!, are no longer thought by their patients to be genuine. Sadly, their now objectively demonstrable genuineness (never mind what their patients think) no longer proves to be therapeutically potent. Objective research has now shown that the whole idea of genuineness as therapeutically important was wrong in the first place! Thus, if such research stumbles across an important feature of psychotherapy which is in fact *not* invariant and mechanical— such as the personal relationship between patient and therapist—it can deal with it only by turning it into nonsense of one kind or another, and ultimately losing it.

The repeated failure of conventional research in psychotherapy to come up with anything like what it expects it should be able to come up with has resulted in a kind of chronic frustration which expresses itself in what one might describe as scientifically degenerate squabbles over research methodology. Countless authorities can be cited for any particular view, countless hypotheses can be advanced to account for any set of data, countless errors of research design and statistical analysis can be advanced to destroy opponents' claims. Somewhere underlying this endless and singularly fruitless process is the myth of the 'crucial experiment': the belief that one day a study will be carried out of such perfect design, such faultless mathematical precision, such impeccable logic and such compelling empirical content as to silence all critics, who will instead be forced into mute reverence for the therapeutic truths revealed.

What psychotherapy research has done, then, is to draw attention to a number of phenomena with which it is not itself equipped to deal. As already stated, these are the phenomena centring on the *personal* nature of the relation between patient and therapist. If these personal themes are to be successfully pursued, it would seem that our research assumptions will have to be modified. Among other things, we shall have to recognize that strict objectivity is impossible, and that what happens in psychotherapy is a function of the perspectives of those involved in it. We shall also have to take account of the fact that therapist, patient, and research worker are all capable of functioning at the same conceptual level and may mutually influence each other. In the absence of any evidence that it is a viable concept in the arena of human affairs, we are also forced to abandon determinism, and we must grapple directly with the complexity of human *meanings* rather than trying to reduce them to scientifically attractive but entirely misleading behavioural or physiological stimuli.

To anticipate later themes for a moment, what this means is that the process of research in psychotherapy, just as the process of therapy itself, is to be seen as one of *co-operation* between researcher and researched (or therapist and patient) in the *negotiation* of a view of therapy which both can share. In the course of our inquiry into these processes we shall be encountering just those 'non-specific' factors in psychotherapy which are thought by patients, and by therapists like Frank, to be of significance: understanding, responsibility, courage, personal influence, and so on.

The scientist is, of course, usually seen as the possessor of great power, the unlocker of secrets which he can then use to bring Nature to her knees. He is not usually seen as having to co-operate with his subject-matter in order to negotiate the 'truth' with it. But then the situation in psychotherapy, and indeed in much of psychology generally, is not a usual one in this sense, and it may be that we have to change our idea of scientific methodology, and, even more drastic, modify our scientific aspirations of 'prediction and control', if we are to remain true to the higher-order scientific ideal of doing justice to our experience, of taking what we find in psychotherapy seriously. It will be our task in the next chapter to consider whether such an undertaking could be considered in any sense scientifically valid.

1 See, for example, A. E. Bergin and S. L. Garfield. (1971). *Handbook of Psychotherapy and Behavior Change.* New York & London: Wiley. Also, J. Meltzoff and M. Kornreich. (1970). *Research in Psychotherapy.* New York: Atherton Press.

2 Eysenck, H. J. (1952). The effects of psychotherapy: an evaluation. *Journal of Consulting Psychology*, **16**, 319.

3 See papers by A. E. Bergin. (1966). Some implications of psychotherapy research for therapeutic practice. *Journal of Abnormal Psychology*, **71**, 235; D. J. Kiesler. (1966). Some myths of psychotherapy research and the search for a paradigm. *Psychological Bulletin*, **65**, 110; S. Rosenzweig. (1954). A transvaluation of psychotherapy: a reply to Hans Eysenck. *Journal of Abnormal and Social Psychology*, **49**, 298.

4 Wolpe, J. (1962). The experimental foundations of some new psychotherapeutic models. In A. J. Bachrach (ed.) *Experimental Foundations of Clinical Psychology.* New York: Basic Books.

5 Fiedler, F. E. (1951). Factor analyses of psychoanalytic, non-directive and Adlerian therapeutic relationships. *Journal of Consulting Psychology*, **15**, 32.

6 Whitehorn, J. C. and Betz, B. J. (1954). A study of the psychotherapeutic relationships between physicians and schizophrenic patients. *American Journal of Psychiatry*, **111**, 321.

7 Much of this work is summarized in C. B. Truax and R. R. Carkhuff. (1967). *Towards Effective Counselling and Psychotherapy: Training and Practice.* Chicago: Aldine.

8 Strupp, H. H., Wallach, M. S. and Wogan, M. (1964). Psychotherapy experience in retrospect: questionnaire survey of former patients and their therapists. *Psychological Monographs*, **78**, no. 11, whole no. 588.

9 See T. M. Caine and D. J. Smail. (1969). *The Treatment of Mental Illness.* London: University of London Press. Also, N. Kreitman. (1962). Psychiatric orientation: a study of attitudes among psychiatrists. *Journal of Mental Science*, **108**, 317; D. J. Pallis and B. E. Stoffelmayr. (1973).

Social attitudes and treatment orientation among psychiatrists. *British Journal of Medical Psychology*, **46**, 75.

10 See for example D. J. Smail. (1970). Neurotic symptoms, personality and personal constructs. *British Journal of Psychiatry*, **117**, 645; F. M. McPherson and A. Gray. (1976). Psychological construing and psychological symptoms. *British Journal of Medical Psychology*, **49**, 73.

11 An interesting start in this direction has been made by T. M. Caine, B. Wijesinghe and R. R. Wood. (1973). Personality and psychiatric treatment expectancies. *British Journal of Psychiatry*, **122**, 87.

12 Sloane, R. B., Staples, F. R., Cristoll, A. H., Yorkston, N. J. and Whipple, K. (1975). *Psychotherapy Versus Behavior Therapy.* Cambridge, Mass. and London: Harvard University Press.

13 Frank, J. D. (1973). *Persuasion and Healing.* Baltimore and London: Johns Hopkins University Press.

14 Bannister, D. (1966). Psychology as an exercise in paradox. *Bulletin of the British Psychological Society*, **19**, 21.

4

The Scientific Philosophy
of Psychotherapy

We inherited, say at the beginning of this century, a notion of the physical world as a causal one, in which every event could be accounted for if we were ingenious, a world characterized by number, where everything interesting could be measured and quantified, a determinist world, a world in which there was no use or room for individuality, in which the object of study was simply there and how you studied it did not affect the object, it did not affect the kind of description you gave of it, a world in which objectifiability went far beyond merely our own agreement on what we meant by words and what we are talking about, in which objectification was meaningful irrespective of any attempt to study the system under consideration. It was just the given real object; there it was, and there was nothing for you to worry about of an epistemological character. This extremely rigid picture left out a great deal of common sense.

The writer of these words,[1] written in 1956, prefaced them with the warning that 'the worst of all possible misunderstandings would be that psychology be influenced to model itself after a physics which is not there any more, which has been quite outdated'. These were not, moreover, the words of some disaffected critic of the scientific orthodoxy, disillusioned with his failure to find a productive corner for himself in the intellectual establishment; they were written in fact by Robert Oppenheimer, prestigious physicist, 'father' of that most awesome example of scientific achievement, the atomic bomb. And yet his warning, like the arguments on which it was based, has largely gone unheeded by behavioural scientists, and, as we have seen in the earlier chapters of this book, the model of science which Oppenheimer characterized as outdated even for physics continues to exercise great, and sometimes damaging, influence on the theory and practice of psychotherapy.

Over and over again, the most compelling features of psycho-therapy are passed over because they do not easily fit in with our conception of what it is to be scientific—we cannot reconcile them with the objective, mechanical, determinate principles with which we feel we must comply if our activities are to be licenced by the

63

authority of Science. As we have seen, this uneasy fit between the experience of psychotherapy and the orthodox scientific framework results in a number of strategies, none of them particularly helpful in furthering our understanding of psychotherapy. One course is simply to crush the phenomena of therapy into their constricting scientific mould, ignore the violence thereby done to them, and recite your scientific credo loudly enough to drown all protests. This, more or less, is the manner of orthodox behaviourism. Or, alternatively, you could decide sadly that psychotherapy cannot really be understood scientifically at all, and relegate it, as Frank appears to do, to the realm of the 'healing arts', awaiting the day when advances in biochemistry or physiology will render the whole business unnecessary anyway. Or again, one can lose patience with the whole intellectual 'scene', decide that science is hopelessly impersonal and dehumanizing anyway, and get on with the job of curing people and fostering their growth unencumbered by any rationalistic claptrap. A number of the 'humanist' psychologists appear to favour this course. Alternatively, and not all that different from this caricature of the 'humanist' solution, one can take what could be called a 'naïve technological' stance, and simply support any therapeutic procedure which seems to 'work', rejecting as tiresome and irrelevant questions about *why* they work, how you know they are *good* for people, and so on. These alternatives exemplify fairly accurately what has happened in the field of psychotherapy, and it is interesting to reflect that the resulting shambles is due almost entirely to the uncritical acceptance of precisely that model of science to which Robert Oppenheimer objects.

But if this is so, why has this scientific model not been abandoned long ago, especially since its weaknesses can seem obvious even to non-psychological scientists like Oppenheimer?

I think it at least plausible that the mechanist/determinist scientific model has dominated, and largely continues to dominate, psychology principally because of the *authority* it confers upon the psychologist. As we saw in the previous chapter, the psychologist, unlike his counterpart in the natural sciences, is dealing with a subject-matter (people) which is capable of answering him back. Not only is he open, as are all scientists, to the questioning and criticism of his expert colleagues, but he is also exposed to the scepticism of the very things he is supposed to be an expert about. One way he can make himself invulnerable to this form of attack is to espouse a philosophy of science which *objectifies* the people he is studying and renders them amenable to prediction and control. Any answering back they then do can easily be dismissed as a failure on their part to recognize the 'true' scientific state of affairs, and he will put his faith in 'behavioural laws' which he feels to be every bit as powerful as the laws of natural science on which, he feels, they are modelled. In other words, in order to escape his fallibility as a *person*—to which he cannot claim to be any less prone than the persons he is studying—he has to associate himself with a body of knowledge which is *im*personal. Having succeeded, in theory, in this enterprise, the psychologist is then caught in the dilemma that he can no longer deal adequately with his subject-matter, which *is* personal.

Perhaps, however, the project to objectify science could be made less attractive to the psychologist if it could be demonstrated that it is in any case not possible, even in the physical sciences; for then he need not feel quite so bad about having to work out an alternative. If, that is, science can be shown *not* to be dealing in cast-iron certainties, its methods *not* sanctioned by the stamp of impersonal reality, we may begin to see ways in which we can come to terms with our personal fallibility.

At this juncture, there are a number of philosophers of science who come to our rescue. Foremost among these is Michael Polanyi, whose book, *Personal Knowledge*,[2] deals precisely with these problems in the context of science generally. In this book, Polanyi demonstrates how all attempts to ground the scientific enterprise on some formal, objective method have failed. The reasoning behind such attempts runs something like this: the universe, or at least enough of it for our purposes, is determined according to the law of cause and effect. If we can find out enough about it at any one point in time, we can then calculate what it will look like at future points. Science then becomes the refinement of the *methods* by which such calculations can be made, and 'being scientific' means rigorously applying these methods to the 'facts' of the universe which are revealed to us. Thus, all we need to do is to discover the rules by which deductions from hypotheses can be tested, proper measurements made, and so on. However, Polanyi shows that none of the rules yet advanced as embodying the scientific method accounts satisfactorily for all of the scientific discoveries we have made. What all of them leave out of account is the *personal activity of the scientist himself.* That such oversights should have been made by 'men of great intellectual distinction' can be explained, Polanyi suggests, by their 'desperate craving to represent scientific knowledge as impersonal'. But, just as we have already noted in the case of the psychologist, the more the scientist succeeds in this project, the more he fails in the total scientific enterprise. As Polanyi puts it: [3]

This is how a philosophic movement guided by aspirations of scientific severity has come to threaten the position of science itself. This self-contradiction stems from a misguided intellectual passion—a passion for achieving absolutely impersonal knowledge which, being unable to recognize any persons, presents us with a picture of the universe in which we ourselves are absent. In such a universe there is no one capable of creating and upholding scientific values; hence there is no science.

The very word 'scientific' is still frequently used to convey a total freedom from values, a noble state of pure objectivity from which our wants, wishes, beliefs and prejudices have been purged by a disinfecting exposure to the rigorous checks of an impersonal reality. The white-coated scientist is seen as a kind of high priest of truth, toughened by his exposure to the cold blast of actuality, immune to the subjective errors of bias and sentimentality to which the rest of us are prone.

Another philosopher of science, Feyerabend, suggests that this picture is a fairy tale: [4]

But the fairy tale is false. . . . There is no special method which guarantees success or makes it probable. Scientists do not solve problems because they possess a magic wand—methodology, or a theory of rationality—but because they have studied a problem for a long time, because they know the situation fairly well, because they are not too dumb (though that is rather doubtful nowadays when almost anyone can become a scientist), and because the excesses of one scientific school are almost always balanced by the excesses of some other school. (Besides, scientists only rarely solve their problems, they make lots of mistakes, and many of their solutions are quite useless.) Basically there is hardly any difference between the process that leads to the announcement of a new scientific law and the process preceding passage of a new law in society: one informs either all citizens or those immediately concerned, one collects 'facts' and prejudices, one discusses the matter, and one finally votes.

The solution to these problems is, then, for the scientist to put himself back into his picture of the world, and to recognize the essential part played in it by his own values, beliefs and commitments. As Polanyi says: [5]

For, as human beings, we must inevitably see the universe from a centre lying within ourselves and speak about it in terms of a human language shaped by the exigencies of human discourse. Any attempt rigorously to eliminate our human perspective from our picture of the world must lead to absurdity.

And again:[6]

If man died, his undeciphered script would convey nothing. Seen in the round, man stands at the beginning and at the end, as begetter and child of his own thought.

It is of course hard for the 'man in the street' to shake off the conviction that the world he perceives around him consists entirely of 'things in themselves', existing completely independently and objectively, and it is perhaps, therefore, not surprising that he is ready to grant the scientist, who appears to be able to penetrate this objective reality, a special kind of knowledge, a knowledge of things as they really are. Once the realization has been made, however, that the way things are cannot sensibly be detached from the way we see them (as Kant also reminded us), we can begin to see that the scientist's knowledge is not an especially privileged insight into reality, but a certain *kind* of knowledge, a particular way (and a particularly human way) of looking at the world.

Science, then, cannot be separated from the people who carry it out, nor can its methods and precepts. The nature of the world is not imposed upon man by virtue of its independent, objective characteristics, but men create a world within which they can perform their scientific operations. In an important sense, the world is man made; the scientist is *responsible* for his picture of the world. The world is discovered in the experience of men, not in the revelation of some kind of final actuality.

What makes the scientific community different from other kinds of human association is the set of values shared by scientists. These probably cannot be stated formally in any very precise way, and almost certainly drift and change with the passage of time. For the most part, scientific values seem to focus on the ways in which *personal* knowledge can be shared and elaborated within the scientific community. Such personal knowledge is not acquired entirely passively through reading books or attending lectures, but rests, as Polanyi points out, on the *active acquaintance* of the scientist with his subject-matter—indeed, the very basis of his knowledge may be quite impossible to verbalize in any adequate manner. In this way the scientist may 'know' something in the same sense that one can be said to 'know' what honey tastes like: such knowledge cannot be acquired or transmitted outside the sphere of personal acquaintance, although it can be shared, and discussed, by those who have experienced it. What allows scientists to construct the intellectual edifice of science is their shared acquaintance with its subject-matter, and their shared evaluation of how to develop their understanding of it. Partly, no doubt, this may involve the use of certain *methods* to which scientists may give their assent, perhaps because, as with the principles of logic or mathematics, they find them *personally* compelling. But science cannot be identified with these methods: logic gives no guarantee of truth, and can be (and has been) associated with extremely unscientific undertakings.

There is, naturally, a sense in which objectivity and agreement are indeed important parts of the scientific value system, but this is not the dogmatic objectivity of behaviourist psychology, which is used as an attempt to *force* a consensus among psychologists. It is, rather, a kind of shared subjectivity. Oppenheimer suggests that the criterion of scientific truth:

> . . . must come from analysis, it must come from experience, and from that very special kind of objectivity which characterizes science, namely that we are quite sure that we understand one another and that we can check up on one another.

For another physicist of great distinction, P. Bridgman,[7] even agreement of this kind becomes problematic, and the core of scientific activity becomes a matter of explaining the relations of individuals to each other:

> I believe that in society as at present constituted the possibility of consensus, except with respect to the simplest situations and as a first approximation, is a mirage. There is no such thing as true consensus, and any ostensible reality supposed to be revealed by the consensus does not exist. To my mind this only underlines the importance of the individual and the importance of understanding the relations of individuals to each other. It also underlines the necessity of making my own report in the first person.

However hard it is to achieve, a central feature of the scientist's personal commitment is what Polanyi calls his 'universal intent', i.e. a commitment to a view of the world as shared. Thus scientists seek and work for objectivity on the basis of their personal acquaintance with their subject-matter; it is not imposed upon them from without, and cannot be set up as a *test* of the validity of scientific statements.

Specifying what scientific, as opposed say to religious, artistic, or indeed technological, values are is in any case by no means a simple task. A significant point seems to be that science seeks ultimately to convince us of a proposition's truth by referring us to evidence which we cannot in good faith deny, and that involves reference to a perceptual and experiential world which we find we have in common. The methodology of science seems, again in part, to be aimed at boiling down our more complex and questionable conceptions to simple and compelling ones.

If we are not to abandon psychology, and the procedures which, like psychotherapy, follow from it, to an undilutedly ethical domain in which theories are believed and practices practised simply because theorists and practitioners like or approve of them, it seems that we must indeed try very hard to find a *scientific* framework for them. And this because scientific statements seem to carry a special kind of conviction which is not arrived at by other routes. If this conviction is not attainable through the formal application of objective, mechanistic methodology, what is its source?

As I have already implied, the conviction which scientific statements carry seems to me to stem not from checking them against evidence from an outside, objective 'reality', but from internal experience. We are convinced because we may, to test our agreement with a scientific proposition, freely and unconstrainedly consult our experience (from 'ourselves as centre', as Bridgman puts it); we are not asked to accept it on faith, or on outside authority. What we do find compelling about scientific statements with which we agree is that we cannot in good faith deny the evidence of our own experience, and this is an experience which takes place *within* ourselves. And what makes this process so attractive is that we are compelled by nothing but our free acceptance of our experience; we *choose* to be bound by it. Just because of this, scientific inquiry carries with it a marked quality of freedom. We do not have to submit to a tyrannical intellectual authority, as in magical or religious systems, nor indeed do we have to accept the overbearing demands of an absolute objectivity. Our commitment to the values of science follows from the trust we have in the evidence of our experience and is willingly self-imposed. Not, of course, that there is anything infallible about personal experience, and it certainly cannot be used as a guarantee of any kind of objective truth or certainty. It does, however, constitute the permission we give ourselves to assent to or dissent from scientific statements.

The authority which the mechanistic psychologist seeks for his pronouncements is, then, a chimera, because the 'objective' world he wants to ground his authority in cannot in any case be divorced from the world of his *personal* experience. He keeps his 'objective' authority at the expense of inventing an impossible world and a pseudo-science.

So that we can understand better the process of psychotherapy, and how it can be investigated scientifically, it is also important to examine a little further what is involved in the kind of objectivity which we *can* accept as valid and this, as we have seen, turns upon the ability of people who are involved in the scientific/ psychotherapeutic exercise being able to agree with each other. Scientists seek consensus, and make conditions for it as favourable as they can by, for example, using the same systems of measurement and agreeing on a common language.

But although consensus is clearly a highly important part of the scientific process, and without it, presumably, there would be no science, it also cannot be made a *criterion* of scientific truth. If, in the case of the natural sciences, our sensory impressions did not *happen* to match (if, for example, we did not all see, even after debate and argument, the same number of coloured patches on a microscopic slide) scientific progress would presumably be impossible; but that does not mean that such progress could be brought about by insisting on a consensus of some artificial kind. Science capitalizes on the happy accident that, in some important respects, human beings share a common experience of the world, and can build an intellectual understanding of it on that basis. If you are wondering who in their right mind would try to bring about an artificial consensus as a substitute for common experience, you do not, unfortunately, have to look far for examples. Much of the dogmatic insistence on 'measurement' in psychology and psychiatry is directed precisely at this end. There are systems of psychiatric diagnosis, for example, which seek a monopoly of the kind of questions people can be asked: thus if *everybody* used a certain diagnostic inventory in precisely the same way, the answers obtained, which of course could only vary within the range set by the questions, would be taken to reflect the presence of real disease entities. Again, there is the personality theorist who appears to try to extend the validity of the dimensions of personality he feels he has isolated by giving them a number in a 'universal index' (which he has in fact created himself). In other words, because one can measure what one can agree about, many psychologists and psychiatrists seem to feel that one can find something to agree about by inventing a system of measurement first and insisting thereafter that people fit their disparate experience into it.

Thus, one does not bring about a scientific result by insisting on consensus, but the consensus comes about through an honest assessment of the degree to which one man's experience coincides with another's. Consensus is in this way a *personal* discovery; we *find* that we agree. Of course, if I see what you do not see, I do not at the outset have to conclude that either of us is wrong: I may first check my own experience to make sure that I am not being misled by some (relatively) fleeting illusion or hallucination. I may even negotiate with you concerning our respective perceptions. But my ultimate check will be against further experience of my own. If I were to abandon my own experience in favour of a wider consensus (based perhaps on a dogmatic assertion of what is 'scientific'), if I were to deny what I see because others say they do not see it, or because in some sense I am not supposed to see it, I should thereby *cease* being scientific.

Truth becomes possible as a concept because we *happen to* share certain important areas of our experience. It is thus a social concept, a way of saying what we have in common; it is to be found in the areas of our private worlds which overlap.

How we come to acquire the rather fundamental kinds of experience which we seem able to share (in particular our experience of the physical world) is obviously an exceedingly complex question, and it is certainly not my intention to suggest that they just happen to be present in some neatly finished form in every new-born infant. They may in fact be the result of complex negotiations between mother and child,[8] and they may vary from culture to culture. On the whole they seem to be relatively stable, and there is a limit set on the degree to which they are negotiable. That limit (though it may vary over time) is defined by the individual's personal acquiescence in them on the basis of what he finds at 'himself as centre'.

One reason, then, why the natural sciences have proved so powerful is because they are built on areas of human experience (basically sense experience) in which it has proved possible to find wide consensus on the basis of personal consent. For science to flourish, however, it is also necessary for men to *value* this approach. If I value scientific truth, I value your free discovery that your experience overlaps mine, and if I value scientific method in a wider sense, I will value the possibilities for communication which this discovery affords us, and the fruits it bears in terms of further elaborations of our experience which we can, at least potentially, share.

I may of course not value these things. I may instead wish to make my views absolute by *insisting* that you see things my way, I may try to impose my 'reality' upon you either by force or by appealing to some other kind of value which I think may persuade you—for example, that my system is effective, or economical, or will achieve the greatest happiness for the greatest number. Appeals of this kind, as we have seen, are often enough to be detected at the heart of various psychotherapeutic approaches, which is all very well as long as they do not continue surreptitiously to be put forward as 'scientific'.

This discussion of the nature of the scientific enterprise introduces no revolutionary new concepts. It simply reasserts a view of science which has been advanced often in the past, frequently, as we have seen, by natural scientists themselves. This view, which can be summed up as making the *personal* role of the scientist *central* to an understanding of his activity has, however, been almost entirely neglected in psychology and psychotherapy, with consequences we have noted already often enough. That such a view of science exists does however suggest that the student or practitioner of psychotherapy can cease glancing nervously over his shoulder at the tablets of the psychological law on which are engraved the dogmas of mechanism, and get on with the business of taking what he finds in his own experience, and that of his patients, seriously.

In many ways this means a depressingly fresh start, in which almost all the assumptions of traditional psychology, whether cherished or simply taken for granted, must be re-examined for the polluting effects they may be having on our psychological understanding and our ability to get to grips with our subject-matter. Because people are people and not things, the science we end up with may well not look very much like what we have come to expect, even if naïvely, from the natural sciences, and we may well find that we have to abandon all hopes of the control and predictability which once looked such an exciting prospect. But if there is disappointment at the failure of the original projects of 'scientific psychology', there may also be relief that we can be freed of its demands for objectivity, generality, and so on, and still remain scientific.

As far as psychotherapy is concerned, the most we can hope for, perhaps, is some understanding of our activities as people in relation to each other (patients and therapists); not, certainly, to predict and control them, but to provide a basis on which we can share experience, talk about what we are doing, and define the limits of our understanding.

Because our experience of ourselves, other people, and of society and the values it enshrines is infinitely more complicated than our experience of the physical world, we cannot expect quickly to find a common language in which we can discuss these issues, or more or less ready-made instruments with which we can measure them. This demands a tolerance of different perspectives, a good will towards the experience of others, a patient groping after shared understandings, which will require a very different spirit from that in which psychological inquiry has largely been carried out in recent decades.

Even if what is required is a fresh start, it is fortunately not so necessary to make it with an entirely clean slate. The methodology of traditional approaches to research and practice in psychotherapy may have blinded many of those involved to the content of what they were dealing with, but the content is nevertheless there, and has, even if often passed over as 'non-specific', occasionally been examined with painstaking care by some observers.

In the chapters which follow an attempt will be made to draw together some of these observations, many of which are not to be found clearly stated in the mainstream of psychotherapeutic inquiry, and to add some of my own. The guiding aim of this inquiry will be to stay as close as possible to psychotherapy as a *personal* activity (and hence to be 'scientific' in the sense advocated in this chapter), and to arrive at an explication of some of its more puzzling features without resorting to the kind of mechanistic dogma which destroys understanding and undercuts experience. I certainly do not have a patented system, or a ready-made methodology, or a final solution to offer. More, I hope, a contribution to a scientific conversation about some aspects of psychotherapy.

1 Oppenheimer, R. (1956). Analogy in science. *American Psychologist*, **11**, 127.
2 Polanyi, M. (1958). *Personal Knowledge*. London: Routledge & Kegan Paul.
3 ibid., p. 142.
4 Feyerabend, P. (1975). *Against Method*. London: NLB.
5 op. cit., p. 3.
6 op. cit., p. 265.
7 Bridgman, P. W. (1959). *The Way Things Are*. Cambridge, Mass.: Harvard University Press.
8 See, for example, J. Shotter. (1974). The development of personal powers. In M. P. M. Richards (ed.). *The Integration of the Child into a Social World*. London: Cambridge University Press.

5

Freedom and Responsibility

If people were no more than complicated machines, it would be reasonable to seek to 'cure' their neuroses by operating technically on whatever caused them. In other words, a mechanistic and deterministic stance towards psychotherapy would be appropriate. Such a stance has, however, been rejected repeatedly in this book. It is now time that the somewhat abstract arguments which have been used to support that rejection are substantiated with rather more concrete suggestions about how we may view the processes of psychotherapy in positive terms. The particular concern of this chapter will be to provide an alternative to determinist explanations of how neurosis comes into being, and how it may be changed. The alternative offered is basically very simple: that is, that neurotic behaviour represents the personal strategies of those who enact it, and is based on free choice. This is by no means a startlingly novel view—we have already seen in Chapter 2 that several psychotherapies hold it in one form or another—but it does confront the thoughful critic with a number of puzzling problems. For example, neurosis involves psychological distress—nobody could *want* to be overcome with panic every time he or she leaves the front door or gets on a bus; nobody could see hour-long rituals of compulsive hand-washing as something he has *chosen* to do. And if these and other neurotic behaviours are something that the person is *responsible* for, why can he not simply 'pull himself together'?

The difficulty with these problems and questions is, I think, that they rest on some grossly over-simplified assumptions contained in our culture. The most blatant of these is that if I do something deliberately and successfully, I am to be congratulated for the actions which I am happy to be responsible for. If, on the other hand, I do things which turn out badly or, more important, which cause me distress, I look for 'causes' outside my own agency which will make my actions 'not my fault'. Again, if I do something bad or distressing, the alternative to its being caused by something outside my control is for it to be seen precisely as being my *fault*. If the

75

neurotic is not ill, he must be a liar, a coward or a con-man.

The task of this chapter, then, is to suggest a way in which we can conceive of neurotic behaviour as the personal responsibility of the individual who enacts it without involving ourselves in simplistic accusations of blame and guilt: for there is one thing which almost (though not quite) all psychotherapists are agreed upon, and that is that blame and exhortation are just about the most fruitless ways to approach psychological disturbance.

The point of this inquiry is no idle philosophical exercise simply to justify a personal dislike of mechanism and determinism. It is, on the contrary, vital to the resolution of one of the most confusing paradoxes of psychotherapy, and one which must surely have puzzled any experienced psychotherapist. For, billed as an expert in the treatment of psychological 'illness', the therapist finds himself occupying a social position—quite possibly in some kind of official institution—in which he is expected to 'do something about' the problems patients bring to him. His very *raison d'être* is based upon what may reasonably be expected of him as a skilled technician. He has degrees and diplomas, and it is considered just that he should be paid for his services. He exists in a culture which defines psychological disturbance as illness, and his very title suggests that it is in the cure of illness that his professional competence lies. And illness is, of course, something for which people can scarcely be held responsible. And yet the therapist soon finds that one of his most central concerns in his activity with his patients is to negotiate with them a view that only they (the patients) can change themselves: he has no psychological spanners with which he can adjust their misery. If they are to change they must *do* something.

Most psychotherapists have to some extent recognized this problem in one form or another, even when they themselves have subscribed to a basically determinist psychology. Freudian psychoanalysis, for example, is greatly preoccupied with the phenomena of 'resistance': the ways, that is, in which patients sabotage and evade the analyst's attempts to interpret their infantile aims and fantasies in a manner which will make open to them the possibility of behaving maturely and responsibly. In dealing with this 'resistance', however, the analyst has a problem, because he has to square what he experiences as the resistance of a *person* with the necessity of staying within the bounds of determinist science. A contemporary psychoanalytic paper[1] states the case for psychological determinism very clearly:

In the first place Freud took over the idea of determinism from the physical sciences and applied it to the psychological sphere. The assumption of psychological determinism is still a cornerstone of psychoanalytic thinking. Briefly, it is the belief that every aspect of behaviour or subjective experience, and every aspect of the functioning of the mental apparatus, can be seen as the outcome of the events (psychological as well as non-psychological) which precede it. It implies that *theoretically* it should be possible to predict and to understand a psychological 'event' in terms of all the forces operative at the time and which have operated in the past. While this is theoretically so, *practically* such precision is impossible, although psychoanalytic psychologists make the assumption that every psychological manifestation or experience stands in a definite and theoretically explicable relationship to the whole of the person's psychological life. Psychological determinism has sometimes been referred to as the principle of *causality*. Determinism is, of course, an assumption which has been generally made in science.

And:

Psychological determinism has sometimes been seen as being in conflict with the idea of 'free will'. This conflict has, on the whole, been exaggerated. An individual may possess a high degree of internal security, and be in a position to exercise his judgment consciously in regard to which of a number of courses he will pursue. Nevertheless, the assumption of psychological determinism could still apply to his final decision, in that one could regard that decision as the outcome of the operation of many factors, including those entering into his assessment and judgment of the situation. However, because of the existence of unconscious mental functioning . . . the psychoanalyst would still take the view that many actions which appear on the surface to be a consequence of free acts of will are inevitably determined by the influence of unconscious psychological forces acting on the individual.

It would be surprising if this formulation did not place the analyst and his patient in an almost impossibly paradoxical situation. If the patient's behaviour is seen as being determined by '*forces*' operating '*on*' him, it seems scarcely reasonable for the analyst to characterize this to him as 'resistance'. And the patient himself might justifiably feel aggrieved at imputations of resistance to his *conduct*, when the theory itself suggests that his conduct is not conduct at all, but reaction to forces operating on him. Of the two, the psychoanalytic concept·of resistance is far more valuable than that of psychological determinism, but to be useful it must be seen in the context of conduct, or activity, for which the patient is responsible. How it can be seen as such will, I hope, become clear as we proceed.

Patients themselves, once they have been through a psycho-therapeutic experience, seem less embarrassed about acknowledging their behaviour as responsible action than is often the case with their therapists. We have already noted in Chapter 3 that successful therapy patients accept the importance of 'facing' problems and 'shouldering responsibility'. Writers on the psychotherapeutic process, even when they agree with this view, are often more cautious, presumably because of their scientific scruples. Frank, in the book already referred to, speaks of the importance in therapy of enhancing the patient's 'sense of mastery', apparently baulking at the prospect of *actual* mastery. Even behaviour therapists have become concerned with the conditioning of 'self-control' responses—showing thereby, perhaps, an admirable regard for the pragmatics of therapy, even if a blithe disregard for theoretical consistency.

In many ways, of course, the Unconscious of psychoanalysis and the conditioned reflex of behaviourism have been created precisely in order to preserve determinism in psychology and psychotherapy. If the psychologist or therapist is to be an expert in something, it must be something in which his subjects or patients are not expert, something which can be known and manipulated by the expert for purposes of prediction and control. Thus, when the analytic patient claims that he is acting for some conscious purpose, he can be told that his actions are 'really' the result of some unconscious wish; he cannot successfully challenge the analyst's view, because only the latter understands the mechanics of unconscious processes. Similarly, the behavioural expert controls the patient by controlling the 'reinforcement contingencies' (the rewards and punishments) which operate upon him.

These theoretical positions are, of course, no more than scientistic bluff. We have already seen that the psychological scientist is not in the same position as he imagines the natural scientist to be. If he attempts to predict and control his subject-matter (people), the latter is perfectly free to observe his operations and out-manoeuvre him. The psychologist can only possibly maintain his position by keeping his scientific theory and method absolutely secret: his predictions can only avoid deliberate refutation by being kept from their objects; his measuring instruments (intelligence and personality tests, etc.) can only be effective if potential subjects are kept in ignorance of their contents. While psychologists can, and do, manage to keep a measure of secrecy about their operations, this is not easy in face-to-face, relatively unstructured procedures like psychotherapy, and patients quickly learn what their therapists are up to. If the therapist resorts to bluff in this situation, if he attempts, as it were, to render his patients amenable to control by suggesting that they are unconscious in a way in which he is not, he is liable rapidly to find his bluff being called. The bluff can most easily be called by the response: 'all right, then, cure me'.

The idea of psychotherapy as a technical operation on the causes of neurosis can in some ways, then, be seen as the upshot of a collusion between treaters and treated. It suits therapists because it accords with their social accreditation as experts, as well as with their idea of what it is to be scientific; it suits patients because the alternative would be for them to feel that their neurosis was their *fault*. This collusive idea is, however, negated in the actual course of psychotherapy, in which therapists find themselves, willy nilly, appealing in some way or other to their patients to take responsibility for themselves and *change* their behaviour, and patients, correspondingly, find themselves with the prospect of having to *do* something.

Partly because of social and cultural expectations, many of which have been deliberately fostered by psychotherapists themselves, and partly because it suits them, patients tend, on initial contact, to present their therapists with *problems*, in the anticipation that the therapist will find the corresponding causes and remove them through technical intervention. The problems which patients present vary in specific terms over a wide range, but in general terms they can perhaps be split into two or three broad categories. Most patients come to the psychotherapist via a chain of medical referrals, originating with the general practitioner and progressing through various contacts with psychiatry. This inevitably means that many of them will have every justification for seeing their problems in terms of illness, and they are likely to couch their description of them in terms of more or less physical symptoms. Anxiety, depression and fear are naturally describable in terms of their physical expression, and these somatic aspects of psychological distress are often what the psychotherapist first hears about. Stomach pains and nausea, headaches, dizziness, dryness of the mouth, palpitations and tension, inexplicable feelings of panic arising apparently out of the blue, uncontrollable weeping, all these are symptoms which may seem relevant to a primarily medical frame of reference, and patients may present them in the expectation that some kind of medical intervention will prove effective. By the time they reach the psychotherapist, however, it is likely that purely medical remedies, such as the use of drugs, will have proved more or less useless. In cases where the problem is cast directly in terms of psychological distress—fear, compulsion, lack of control, etc.—patients are likely to adopt a further hypothesis offered them by the experts: namely, that there is something causing their problem and that, if 'it' can be discovered, the problem will somehow go away. In this respect, they may expect the therapist to discover some forgotten childhood trauma buried deep in 'the subconscious', some psychological violence done them by their family, some deep-seated fear of which they are unaware, the unearthing of which will, like lancing a boil, cause the distress to evaporate.

It is, therefore, often with surprise and resentment that patients learn that matters are not that simple; that, for instance, an understanding of the history and origination of a complaint does not automatically remove it, or that there is no wonder-drug for the removal of their symptoms. They may be puzzled and hostile if the therapist responds to their presentation of the problem by probing into its meaning for them, rather than by accepting it at face value and launching straight into a course of 'treatment'. If, further, he suggests that the significance of the problem may lie in what it is *achieving* for them, hostility may turn to outrage, and rejection of the whole therapeutic enterprise. As Landfield puts it:[2]

A psychotherapist who wishes to convince people that each person must bear some responsibility for his problems as well as his cure works against heavy odds. His underprivileged patients learn early that life has limitations. They also learn that treatment for them is largely custodial and medical. His more privileged clients do learn that professionals will talk with them about their problems. However, they also learn from the pamphlets circulated by associations for mental health that an emotional problem is sickness . . . for which the person is often not responsible. A corollary to this type of logic suggests that if one is not responsible for one's problem, then one assuredly cannot be held responsible for one's own cure. To further complicate the therapist's task of encouraging his clients to assume more responsibility for their lives, the 'body' theorists attribute the cause of behaviour to genetics and spleen, while the 'environmentalists' attribute cause to external circumstances.

This, then, is the predicament commonly faced by the psycho-therapist who is willing to remain true to his experience. He has to convince his patients that their neurosis is something to do with their own agency, something which can only be changed through their acceptance of responsibility for it.

The predicament has not gone unrecognized. One approach quite widely adopted by therapists is to negotiate some kind of 'contract' with patients, in which the aims of treatment, as well as their own responsibilities, are stated as clearly as possible at the outset. In the hospital setting, for example, Cooklin[3] has suggested how staff and patients may initiate the therapeutic process by examining and exposing any unrealistic expectations of passive 'cure', and agreeing aims of treatment which, with his active participation, it may be possible for the patient to achieve. Scott[4] gives an account of the problems presented by the 'medical' expectations which patients often have. He sees these as bearing closely upon patients' wishes to see themselves as not responsible for their problems, but rather as victims of illness, of society, or of the family. He suggests ways in which the hospital ward setting can be designed to counter these expectations, or 'barriers to treatment', as he calls them, and lead to more adaptive and successful strategies. Staff may, for example, avoid 'doing things for' patients *as if* they were ill, or not responsible, and may resist also any attempt made by patients' families to define the hospitalized member's behaviour as 'sick' rather than, in some sense, intentional.

Which brings us back to the problem we must now face squarely. How can somebody want, or intend, to be psychologically disturbed? Can we justify a rejection of the humane notion of 'mental illness' and its replacement by a notion of personal responsibility?

No one, I think, would wish to maintain that an individual is neurotic 'on purpose', in the naïve meaning of that expression. It is, nevertheless, a common experience of psychotherapists that patients *resist* getting better, and it is greatly to Freud's credit that he gave so much attention to this phenomenon. The resistance may be encountered, for example, in the form of patients failing to conform with suggestions from the therapist about how their treatment might be furthered (such suggestions might centre on things they *could* do easily enough, like keeping a diary of troubling events or symptoms, or learning relaxation techniques at home), or might simply be experienced in patients' failure to keep appointments, especially at times when some improvement seemed to the therapist to be imminent. Yet this does not seem to be a matter of simple dishonesty: there seems somehow to be *both* an apparently genuine wish to 'get better' *and* an apparently genuine resistance to getting better when it seems possible to do so. While the resistance may be *denied* by the patient (again apparently genuinely) his actions appear *undeniably* to be aimed intelligently, and often tenaciously, at just such resistance.

Perhaps a concrete example might at this stage help to clarify much of what has been said so far, as well as aid subsequent discussion. As in other clinical examples used in this book, it is based on my own experience, but for obvious reasons does not constitute an accurate account of the problems or circumstances of any one particular individual.

A young, attractive woman complains that she is sexually frigid. She has three small children (conceived in the interests of procreation only) and a husband who is sympathetic and understanding, and whom she 'loves very, very much'. He is the only person she has ever slept with, and they were married at an early age. She has never enjoyed sex positively, either before or since marriage, although once, when they were on holiday in the Canary Isles, it was half-way bearable. Apart from getting no pleasure from sex, she finds it painful. Her first explanatory hypothesis is a physical one: she believes that she must be 'too small inside'. She goes to her general practitioner, who sends her to a gynaecologist. The latter examines her and assures her that she is anatomically normal. She goes back to her general practitioner who prescribes drugs 'to help her relax'. These are to no avail, so her doctor sends her to a psychiatrist, who prescribes different drugs. These do not help either. The psychiatrist now refers her to a psychotherapist who suggests that she come to a therapeutic group. She attends the group for six months. Both she and the group members are puzzled by her complaint: she is not unduly prudish or sexually inhibited in any obvious way, though she reflects that her parents are on the puritanical side, and that sex was a taboo subject at home. Examination of this in the group is exhaustive, but discussion of the problem, in which she herself shows no undue embarrassment, leads to no improvement. A few weeks later she reveals, with considerable hesitancy and pain, that she was 'interfered with' by an elderly male relative at the age of five or six. The group members accept this revelation sympathetically, and one or two of the other women in the group confess to similar experiences. For some weeks this new information is examined for its significance in terms of what it may have done to her relations with men, and some discussion attaches to the rather seductive and yet rejecting, 'teasing' way she relates to the men in the group. This seems to clear the air a lot, but there is still no change in her sex life with her husband. After six months, the patient, the group and the therapist all feel that the best approach would be for her to have some marital counselling, together with her husband. The method to be tried involves discussion, as well as some quite practical counselling on sexual technique, as pioneered by Masters and Johnson.[5] She is enthusiastic about this, and consequently the therapist meets her and her husband for weekly sessions.

At this point, having in previous months run through a series of hypotheses about what 'it' could be, the first signs of resistance begin to emerge. The patient finds reasons why the sexual exercises to be conducted with her husband cannot take place, although there is a week between therapy sessions in which to find time for them. Her husband strikes the therapist as an exceptionally tolerant and understanding man, who is doing conscientiously everything he can to co-operate in treatment. He is somewhat bemused by the development of his wife's apparent lack of enthusiasm, especially after her initial keenness. The therapist encourages the couple to continue, feeling that the wife's problem may simply be some fleeting embarrassment about the project. The following week she telephones the therapist asking him to see her on her own, to which he agrees. At this interview she bursts into tears (which she has never done before) and says that she has come to see her problem in an entirely new light. She is not sexually frigid and, she now realizes, never was. She does not love her husband, and never has. She finds him physically repulsive. She does love the next door neighbour, however, and always has. Nothing has passed between them, but whenever she sees him, her knees 'turn to jelly'. She realizes that she kept herself from recognizing the problem because of what it entailed: she does not want to become involved in the upheaval of breaking up her marriage—she has nowhere to go (as far as she can tell the next door neighbour is quite happy as he is), and she does not want to destroy the happiness of her three children, who love their father.

Suddenly, then, a 'symptom' becomes an acknowledged problem of relationship, an agonizing difficulty, but in no way a mechanical breakdown—either physical or psychological. Moreover, the realization of her predicament burst upon this woman like a bomb—up to that point her search for 'causes' had been as diligent as that of all those who, for a total of seven or eight months, had been therapeutically involved with her, and only the threatening 'cure' of her frigidity with her husband led to her recognition of the true state of her affairs. The 'cure', naturally, had to be resisted, as there was no real problem to which it corresponded: she was not 'frigid' at all. Her 'frigidity', as long as it was left in peace, did, however, serve to keep her from an infinitely more difficult, though in no way pathological, predicament. Somehow or other, her left hand had managed to keep her right hand from getting to grips with that predicament, until the strategy became exposed by the direct challenge posed by marital counselling.

Somehow, then, and often in neurosis, a person may conceal from himself the motives of his own behaviour: he can attribute to external causes behaviour which is in fact purposive or intentional, and so escape responsibility for it.

To understand how this is possible, we have to correct the idea that *actions* are things which we perform in the full light of awareness, things to which *conscious* intentions and motives are particularly appropriate, while things we do 'without knowing why' are the automatic products of causes which we carry round like stones inside us, or which are imposed upon us by outside influences, and for which we cannot be answerable. In fact, satisfactory elucidations of this problem are readily available in the work of a number of philosophers, particularly those of the existentialist school. Much of what follows leans heavily on these ideas, and in particular on the views expressed by Jean-Paul Sartre in his *Being and Nothingness*.

The central point made in this context by Sartre, and others, is that human activity cannot be divorced from its *meaning*, and its meaning involves its *intention*. An action without a meaning ceases to be an action at all, but becomes simply a meaningless movement. Actions, moreover, do not have to be carried out consciously—indeed, much of our meaningful, intentional activity is carried out without any conscious deliberation on our part. This is fairly obvious with trivial activities like combing one's hair or changing gear while driving, but is also true of the much broader 'projects' in which one might be engaged—I live my life as though it had meaning, but would be hard put to it to say what the meaning was. Movements have a quite different quality from voluntary action. If you jog my elbow, my spilling coffee on your carpet can scarcely be seen as involving intentional behaviour on my part. Acts are intentional, movements are caused. If, then, you wish to replace intentions with causes (as, for example, the behaviourist would) you render action meaningless. This, in many respects, is precisely what the neurotic tries to do: to negotiate a view of his activity as meaningless movement. Such a strategy is only persuasive if we insist that activity has to be consciously acknowledged.

To say that activity need not be consciously acknowledged is not to say that it must therefore be unconsciously caused. The activity *is* its meaning and its intention. We split off our intentions from our actions only when we reflect about them, and this is in many ways an artificial process. It is only when we reflect upon our activity that we ascribe conscious motives and intentions to it; we treat what is in fact an integral part of our action as if it were an antecedent cause of it because, after we have done something, we can see that we had reasons for doing it. Sartre states the case as follows: [6]

... it is in fact impossible to find an act without a motive but ... this does not mean that we must conclude that the motive causes the act; the motive is an integral part of the act. For as the resolute project toward a change is not distinct from the act, the motive, the act, and the end are all constituted in a single upsurge. Each of these three structures claims the two others as its meaning. But the organized totality of the three is no longer explained by any particular structure...

Conscious motives and intentions are, then, constructs we invent to account for what we *have* done, they are not things which we necessarily have to consider *before* we can act. (I have on several occasions found it of practical help to make this point to patients who are poised on the edge of a rather anxiety-arousing course of action, but who interpose between themselves and it the necessity for 'making a decision', which they then find they are unable to do; which perhaps goes to show that philosophical points are not necessarily irrelevant to immediate practical concerns.) Action, in fact, must come before deliberation in at least one important sense, as Shotter makes clear: [7]

... before anything can be done with reason and deliberation it must first be done spontaneously; it is only as natural agents, not as self-directing persons, that we could discover any entirely new potential within ourselves. We cannot direct ourselves towards their discovery, as there is no way of knowing, before they are actualized, what our potentialities are. It takes what we have always suspected it takes ... courage. For to actualize new potentials we have to cast ourselves into new situations, suffer the effects they have upon us, and counter them as best we can—all the time, as mere spectators, observing ourselves and noting the results, being determined the next time the situation arises to do deliberately that which in this situation was successful spontaneously.

Here, then, is an observation fundamental to our problem: viz., that, despite superficial subjective impressions, human action does not always follow deliberation, and quite often the explanations we give for our actions have to be found (almost invented) after the event. In this way, we frequently cast around for reasons for our actions much as we might for reasons for the actions of others. We arrest ourselves in mid flight in order to justify our course so far, and, having done so, we delude ourselves if we are not careful that our justifications are causes, and that our behaviour has all along been consciously planned. Of course, it *is* possible to plan one's behaviour before enacting it, but that does not mean that one always does, neither does it make the plan a cause. And even in the case of planned activity, the *reasons* for planning it this way or that need not be, and indeed often are not themselves clear or explicit (in the case of obsessional behaviour, for example, long chains of carefully planned activity can be carried out for reasons which are totally obscured).

As Sartre points out, deliberation, far from being the ultimate source of our activity, the mainspring lying at its centre, need be no more than a relatively unimportant stage in our reflecting over our actions. And even when we do appear to will an action deliberately, there lies behind that will, as he says, 'a more profound intention' of which we are not aware. Consciousness of one's actions is always in the setting of a 'project' which is not conscious of itself in the same sort of way. Our ultimate projects are achieved, Sartre argues, by our living them, not reflecting about them. Much of *Being and Nothingness* makes somewhat impenetrable reading. The following passage, however, makes the point clearly enough:

I can assume consciousness of myself only as a particular man engaged in this or that enterprise, anticipating this or that success, fearing this or that result, and by means of the ensemble of these anticipations, outlining his whole *figure*. Indeed it is thus that I am apprehending myself at this moment when I am writing; I am not the simple perceptive consciousness of my hand which is making marks on the paper. I am well in advance of this hand all the way to the completion of the book and to the meaning of this book—and of philosophical activity in general—in my life. It is within the compass of this project (i.e. within the compass of what I am) that there are inserted certain projects toward more restricted possibilities such as that of presenting this or that idea in this or that way or of ceasing to write for a moment or of paging through a volume in which I am looking for this or that reference, etc. Nevertheless it would be an error to believe that there is an analytical and differentiated consciousness corresponding to this global choice. My ultimate and initial project—for these are but one—is, as we shall see, always the outline of a solution of the problem of being. But this solution is not first conceived and then realized; we *are* this solution. We make it exist by means of our very engagement, and therefore we shall be able to apprehend it only by living it. Thus we are always wholly present to ourselves; but precisely because we are wholly present, we cannot hope to have an analytical and detailed consciousness of what we are. [8]

Our activity, then, in so far as it is activity and not meaningless movement, is saturated everywhere with intention, as an integral part of it, whether or not we recognize it consciously.

The therapist's first task must then be to decide whether his patient's behaviour is activity or merely movement. The latter alternative is certainly not impossible—it may be that the nervous tic which a patient complains of is the result of organic disease interfering with his motor activity and thereby rendering aspects of it meaningless. If, however, the therapist decides that the patient's behaviour does indeed represent activity, his job then becomes one of helping the patient to investigate what he is *intending* by it, and to see that his conscious protestations and justifications, when these conflict with the intention of his actions, have in fact no impelling claim to be considered as more real or more genuine than, or in any way necessarily prior to or invalidating, the 'intending behaviour'.

A patient's activity, then, whether or not he is aware of it, has a meaning which can only be understood in terms of its intention. He has *reasons* for behaving the way he does, and while reasons may be a certain kind of cause, they are not causes in the sense of inexorable forces operating on the individual—they are causes he chooses. Passive reflection is by no means the best method of discovering what one's intentions are—one has to learn to read off the meaning of one's activity (its intention) in much the same way as one reads the intentions of others, i.e. by observing the effects of their behaviour on the world around them. The relation between action and reflection is of course a complex one, and in our observation of ourselves we are constantly interpreting and reinterpreting the meaning of our actions (especially when they do not turn out very successfully). We shall be examining this problem in a little more detail in the next chapter, largely because it is a problem which lies at the very heart of neurosis: it is in the way we explain to ourselves the meaning of our actions that we have the greatest opportunities for self-deception. But for the moment, enough may have been said for us at least to be able to accept that it is by no means obvious that we can expect to *know* what the intentions of our actions are.

Of course the neurotic does not *want* the distressing mental and physical experiences to which his anxiety gives rise, but at the same time it is necessary to recognize that they are the result of strategies which he is carrying out, and which are directed at a certain end. This is by no means to say that he wants to suffer for, say, masochistic reasons, but rather that the broader intention of his activity inevitably involves suffering. In order to avoid social confrontations (an aim which, for one reason or another, he is unable to acknowledge), he, as it were, makes use of the bodily accompaniments of anxiety (tension, gastric pain, etc.) to turn his fear into an *illness* which provides a social justification for not going to parties, facing difficult situations at work, and so on. Absence of the physical distress he experiences would, in other words, bring him face to face with a kind of distress he would be much less willing to experience. He clings on to his symptoms not out of any bloody-minded stubbornness (which perhaps the notion of 'resistance' is liable to evoke) but because he has very good reasons to do so. In order to change, he must find equally good reasons for abandoning his symptoms, and that is why he cannot simply 'pull himself together'. Being unable to change at the drop of a hat does not, therefore, imply that your behaviour is hopelessly determined by leaden causes, but that you have very good reasons—of which you do not have to be aware—for staying the way you are.

It is of course true that *seeing* that you have good reasons for being the way you are may go some way to convincing you of the *possibility* of change, and this presumably is the value of 'insight' in psychotherapy. But on its own it is not enough. Moreover, seeing what your reasons are may not even be essential to change. Accepting that you *have* reasons, even though you can't identify them, may be the more essential first step towards change. This can, I think, be cast in terms of *accepting responsibility* for your conduct, even though you don't know *why* you do it.

In some ways, to ask somebody to accept responsibility for conduct they do not themselves understand may not be such an unusual request as it appears. It is not uncommon, for example, for a person to accept responsibility for a *mistake*. Mistakes are not something we make *on purpose*, and yet we still make them—if we are not ourselves responsible for them, who is? Again, if babies and small children were not held responsible for their actions, they would be unlikely to develop the kinds of skills we expect from them as adults.

In this way, perhaps, we can draw an analogy between neurotic behaviour and the behaviour of children which may go some way to clarifying the relation between responsibility and blame. This is particularly important if we are to provide an acceptable alternative to the 'illness' model of neurosis, that is, one which does not result in inhumane (and obviously inaccurate) accusations that neurosis is the individual's 'own fault'.

We do not expect small children to develop motor co-ordination and social skill without practice. We therefore do not *blame* them for being physically clumsy or socially gauche. And yet we *do* expect them to identify the source of such behaviour (as their own), and in this respect to acknowledge responsibility for it. A child who breaks a teapot because he is more interested in looking out of the window than attending to the angle of the tray (involved, that is, in a broader project than that of clearing the table, but one which nevertheless has consequences for the success with which the latter is done) may not be blamed for breaking it, but nevertheless may be forcefully reminded that it was he who did it. In this way, too, the adult readily recognizes the absurdity of the child's claim that 'it wasn't me', and will probably reflect that that claim stems from a fear of blame. In many ways this is precisely the position of the neurotic who fears that his behaviour, if seen as *his*, will carry an immediate imputation of blame. And yet, of course, he cannot be blamed any more than the child for behaviour over which, though he is responsible for it, he has not yet gained mastery.

The person, then, is responsible for his neurotic behaviour, and has good reasons for it. Having accepted this, he then has to *do* something about it; as well as developing reasons for abandoning it, he will have to involve himself actively in overcoming it, in mastering it.

Just as it is possible, through reflection, to delude oneself about one's intentions, so it is possible to delude oneself that one can change one's intentions reflectively in a way which will result in new activity. 'Knowing what the problem is' does not, in other words, automatically enable the person to deal effectively with it. The foundering of New Year resolutions provides a common example of this observation. To challenge his symptoms, face his fears, learn new social skills, requires that the neurotic confront them *bodily*, and no amount of rumination can achieve this for him. And what he needs above all for this is *courage*.

If we were simply the victims of causes operating upon us, we should not need courage to deal with what we find psychologically distressing—we should simply need to seek out technical help in getting the causes of our behaviour identified and changed. Since, however, neurotic behaviour involves intentional activity, only the person himself can change it, and that requires effort (courage) on his part. The therapist's role in this then becomes not one of technical manipulation—*he* does not change the patient—but one of *encouragement* (here again one is reminded of the words used by patients themselves when describing what they find useful in psychotherapy).

In many respects this provides a more satisfactory theoretical framework in which to place what have largely been seen as therapeutic techniques than that afforded by traditional psycho-therapeutic and behavioural theories, since it reflects more closely what actually happens in therapy. The methods of behaviour therapy—systematic desensitization, social skills training, and so on—can in this way be seen as procedures of encouragement rather than as conditioning techniques, and indeed in this respect behaviour therapy has a great deal to offer. Such methods open up to the patient ways in which he can confront his problems bodily and deal with them actively and directly. Once we have jettisoned the simplistic dogma of science it is supposed to support, the behaviour therapist's emphasis on *behaviour* is in this way crucial, since it enables us to recognize the therapeutic necessity for the patient actually to do something, to operate actively on his experience. This is certainly an important advance on the idea that changes are made by juggling with the intrapsychic contents of the person's 'unconscious'.

There is perhaps a sense in which the procedures whereby a therapist may encourage a patient to get to grips with his predicament, to challenge his fears and actively to experience their resolution, may be seen as technical, but technical in a weak sense. They do not reflect laws of behaviour or the determining influence of conditioned reflexes, but may be seen as flexible strategies which may or may not prove useful to the individual, and they must always be set in the context of the meaning he attaches to them. The bather may deal with the cold sea either by inching into it gradually (behavioural 'systematic desensitization') or by plunging in headlong (behavioural 'implosion'). The method he chooses depends on him, and to elevate either to *the* method would cause a lot of people a good deal of discomfort (not to mention the fact that it is also possible to stay on the beach, or to reserve one's bathing for heated swimming pools).

The therapist who sees his role as purely technical is likely to approach his patients with a kind of psychological tool-kit which, once he has exhausted its capabilities without success, will leave him despairingly bereft of ideas. On the other hand, the therapist who sees his 'technical' activity as flexibly in the service of the general aim of encouragement, will be able to adapt his strategies to the unique set of meanings generated in the relationship between himself and his patient—he will be able to make new tools without, for example, worrying about whether they conform to specifications established by the 'laws of behavioural science'. As long as they fit in with the patient's personal set of meanings, as long as *he* can use them, they will fill the bill quite adequately.

The patient who has the courage to face his problems, to confront them bodily, will discover his freedom to change in his own experience, and will acquire reasons for behaving in ways that he had formerly felt not to be possible. He may also, of course, opt for staying as he was before, but if so he can no longer deceive himself that he is not responsible for doing so—the choice is freely his.

All this, naturally enough, has implications also for the ethics of psychotherapy. If both therapist and patient are looked upon as each independently responsible for their own conduct—whether or not they are able consciously to specify their aims—it becomes, as we have seen, impossible to characterize psychotherapy as a technical procedure. The therapist becomes a guide rather than an expert, a fellow investigator rather than an authority. While he will certainly have influence, his job is not to influence his patients towards any *particular* ends, but to help them acknowledge their own freedom, to recognize that the responsibility for what they do resides with them, and not him. It is unlikely that anyone who accepts the validity of this standpoint will be particularly concerned with the removal of 'symptoms'. 'Illness' behaviour is likely to be seen as strategic, and the therapist will be much more interested in what the patient *means by* his symptoms than he will in simply removing them mechanically. Indeed, he will recognize that, unless there are compelling reasons to believe that the patient's symptoms are in the strict sense unintentional and without meaning (because physically caused, for example), it would be absurd for him to try to remove them.

The therapist must also recognize that he is himself inevitably subscribing to a moral standpoint, i.e. that it is *right* for him to lead people towards a recognition of their freedom. Whether this is a worthier aim than that of, say, conditioning people to being contented and productive members of society, 'adjusted' in their work and play, is entirely debatable. But it is not a less *valid* aim in the sense of being less scientifically respectable or credible. Indeed, that people *are* free, that their behaviour is not simply determined by their biochemistry or conditioned through their 'reinforcement history', conforms more closely to the experience of psychotherapy, and hence to the model of science developed in the previous chapter, than do many competing views.

The therapist who adopts this viewpoint and this moral position is likely to be less concerned than many about what patients do *with* their freedom, and will be prepared for therapeutic outcomes which a few years ago, if not now, might have been frowned upon in more conventional psychiatric circles. A patient may, for example, come to see his or her marriage as hopeless, and get divorced; a person who expresses a wish initially to be 'rid' of homosexual feelings or behaviour may come to accept and value them.

Because of his belief that people's 'wants' and 'needs' are not necessarily a total account of their intentions, such a therapist is unlikely to accept patients' initial versions of their predicament at face value, and he will always run the risk of events unfolding during therapy which were not foreseeable. The most alarming possibility he has to envisage is perhaps that of a patient's suicide. It is clearly possible that a person could come, through therapy, to see that his 'neurosis' was hiding from him a set of circumstances which he now finds unbearable, and that suicide is a solution within the range of his capabilities. Few therapists are likely to see a patient's choice of suicide as a satisfactory solution, however, and this suggests that there may be more to therapy than *just* encouraging people to accept responsibility for themselves. In recognizing that he is responsible for his own conduct as much as patients are for theirs, the therapist is likely to make use of his experience to arrive at judgments about what a patient might do with his freedom in cases where a highly negative outcome seems possible, and to decide whether or not he should enter into therapy with him. He does not, after all, have to apply his theoretical and moral position absolutely inflexibly, and where neurosis hides a predicament of possibly unbearable proportions, he may decide that practical help and support may be of greater value than encouraging its recognition.

The suggestion here that therapists are not responsible *for* their patients, but only for their own conduct towards them, by no means lets them off any moral hooks. Indeed, feeling that you are responsible for what you do with people may make you considerably more concerned and cautious than feeling that you are directly responsible for them or for what they do. In the latter case you would place your trust in your technical skill in controlling the patient manipulatively; in the former you have to recognize that he is free to use your influence in ways you might not be able to anticipate.

1 Sandler, J., Dare, C. and Holder, A. (1972). Frames of reference in psychoanalytic psychology. III A note on the basic assumptions. *British Journal of Medical Psychology*, **45**, 143.
2 Landfield, A. W. (1975). The complaint: a confrontation of personal urgency and professional construction. In D. Bannister (ed.). *Issues and Approaches in the Psychological Therapies*. London and New York: Wiley.
3 Cooklin, A. I. (1974). Exploration of the staff-patient 'contract' in an acute female admission ward. *British Journal of Medical Psychology*, **47**, 321.
4 Scott, R. D. (1973). The treatment barrier. *British Journal of Medical Psychology*, **46**, 45.
5 Masters, W. H. and Johnson, V. E. (1970). *Human Sexual Inadequacy*. Boston: Little Brown.
6 Sartre, J.-P. (1969). *Being and Nothingness*. Trans. H. E. Barnes. London: Methuen, p. 437. Reprinted by permission of Philosophical Library, Inc. Copyright © 1956 by Philosophical Library, Inc.
7 This quotation is taken from an article (*Psychology and Psychotherapy Association Forum*, 1974) which is not generally available. Shotter has however written a very readable book which covers this and related issues in philosophical psychology: Shotter, J. (1975). *Images of Man*. Methuen Essential Psychology series.
8 op. cit., p. 462.

6

Self-Awareness and Self-Deception

In the previous chapter we considered how a person may be engaged in intentional activity while genuinely believing that his behaviour is due to causal factors beyond his control. In this way, there is a contrast between his actual activity and what he tells himself about the reasons for it. In this chapter we shall consider a related phenomenon: instead of looking at the reasons *why* a person behaves the way he does, we shall look at *what* he does, and how what he does appears to him as he reflects upon it.

In the discussion which follows we shall be examining the conditions under which a person may be said to *know* what he is doing, the main point being that sometimes he does and sometimes he doesn't, but that there is in any case no reason why he always should. Much of the time, in other words, we do *not* know what we are doing, and that in itself is neither unusual nor alarming.

Clarification of this issue is essential to an understanding of neurosis, for one of the most frequent strategies employed by neurotic individuals is to maintain that they are not doing what they appear to be doing, or, alternatively, that not knowing what you are doing constitutes an unusual or unsatisfactory state of affairs characteristic, for example, of illness. To complicate matters further, the fact that people *can*, in certain circumstances, know what they are doing is taken in some brands of psychotherapy to suggest that knowing what you are doing is a good thing. I shall argue that this, unless suitably qualified, is unfortunate.

Any psychotherapist with experience of neurotic patients is likely to have been impressed again and again by the extreme incongruity which often arises when a comparison is made between what a patient is doing and what he or she professes to be doing. The significance of the person's activity seems, that is, to be lost on the person himself. The ways this can take place vary, but at times the incongruity is so great that the therapist can barely resist the impression that deliberate deception is involved. For example, a woman claims that she has a 'phobia' of choking, and so is unable to eat anything solid. Her greatest fear, she says, would be occasioned by eating boiled sweets. And yet she arrives for only her second therapy session with a peppermint boiled sweet rattling cheerfully against her teeth. She does not claim to have improved, and is still as afraid as ever of choking. When asked about the sweet in her mouth she looks somewhat puzzled for a while, and then answers blandly that peppermints 'don't really count'.

Again, one can be faced with the kind of incongruity shown in the behaviour of some 'anorexic' patients, who may be resorting to the subtlest of subterfuges in hiding food or otherwise contriving not to eat it, but at the same time showing genuine terror at the prospect of approaching death from starvation. Less dramatic, perhaps, but no less puzzling, is the frequency with which patients simply fail to make connexions between their own activity and what, from their point of view, 'happens to' them. The man who is assailed by nausea every time he is due to become involved in a social engagement, and who is prepared to undergo surgery rather than consider the meaning of his predicament, even though the latter seems obvious to everybody but him; the woman who 'inexplicably' wanders off and loses her memory every time her mother and her husband fall foul of each other; the flamboyant redhead who becomes almost incoherently anxious and bemused after being sexually assaulted by three different men in the space of as many months, and yet still persists in the highly seductive behaviour which presumably led to the incidents in the first place. In its own way compulsive behaviour—rituals of washing or dressing, for example—is equally puzzling. The person 'knows' that his behaviour is 'silly', the fears on which it is based not really justified, and yet he feels compelled to persist. If he cannot simply *stop* washing his hands, must it not be because he is ill?

Our task, then, is to justify the suggestion that there is nothing fundamentally unusual or qualitatively different from normal about such incongruities as these, *except* that the neurotic is making a special kind of use of what is in fact a familiar condition of human psychology.

The classic psychological explanation of how somebody can be doing something of which he himself remains in ignorance is that offered by Freud in his concept of 'repression'. For one reason or another—usually because recognition of what he is doing would prove painful or threatening to his self-esteem—the person is protected from confrontation with the real nature of his enterprises through the operation of a defence mechanism which 'represses' its significance, i.e. renders it 'unconscious'. Freud distinguished between two types of repression: 'primal repression' and 'repression proper'. In the case of primal repression, unconscious mental contents are prevented from becoming conscious through the activity of a kind of mental 'censor', a metaphorical watchman who stands at the gates of the conscious mind with the purpose of rejecting or ejecting unacceptable ideas or impulses which seek to find their way into consciousness. Repression proper is the process by which contents of the conscious mind can be made unconscious. This is achieved by their having withdrawn from them the mental energy needed to keep them conscious.

Stated in this somewhat bald manner, there is clearly rather a simplistic mechanism about the concept of repression which leaves a number of important questions unanswered. How, for example, are the decisions to reject unconscious contents made, and how is withdrawal of mental energy achieved? What, indeed, does 'mental energy' consist of? How do unconscious mental contents exercise an influence over the person's actual activity? Unsatisfactory though Freud's answers to these questions may often seem to present-day psychologists, he does, in one particular passage,[1] elucidate the problem in a way which foreshadows a number of modern approaches, and which may considerably aid our own discussion:

We now seem to know all at once what the difference is between a conscious and an unconscious presentation. The two are not, as we supposed, different registrations of the same content in different psychical localities, nor yet different functional states of cathexis [mental energy] in the same locality; but the conscious presentation comprises the presentation of the thing plus the presentation of the word belonging to it, while the unconscious presentation is the presentation of the thing alone. . . . Now, too, we are in a position to state precisely what it is that repression denies to the rejected presentation in the transference neuroses: what it denies to the presentation is translation into words which shall remain attached to the object. A presentation which is not put into words, or a psychical act which is not hypercathected, remains thereafter in the *Ucs* [Unconscious] in a state of repression.

What Freud is saying, put simply, is that we can behave unconsciously as long as we do not attach words to what we are doing. What he fails perhaps to stress is that this is by no means only a pathological process, and that, furthermore, when we do succeed in attaching words to our activity, when we give a reflective account of what we are doing, the result is frequently for us to mislead ourselves as well as others.

Experience is prior to language. Language elaborates and reveals our experience and allows us to operate upon it, but just as it can be used positively in this way, so it can be used negatively by misidentifying the significance of our experience. This negative use of reflection is particularly evident when we seek to transform an understanding of what we are doing into a kind of *identity*.

This latter point is made particularly convincingly by Sartre in *Being and Nothingness*, where he develops his concept of 'bad faith'. What people *are*, Sartre says, lies in their pre-reflective, continuously unfolding activity, and what they *say* they are can only be a particular version of themselves which they are offering for public, or even merely their own, consumption. What I say I am is always set in a broader activity in which I am engaged, and which I cannot at the same time comment upon; the 'I' of 'I am . . .' is always beyond what it is claiming to be, standing apart from it, so to speak. Therefore, when I claim for myself some particular identity, or when I try to give some kind of total account of myself, I cannot escape misleading, and being misled—I am in 'bad faith'.

Not only, then, is it not unusual for people to do things without being able to give an account of what they are doing, but for them to succeed in doing so with any completeness is not even possible. As Harré and Secord put it:[2]

The standpoint from which one monitors one's monitoring of a performance, from which one gives commentaries upon the way one is doing something and with what aim, is not itself capable of figuring in an account, given from that standpoint. The commentator himself is not capable of description as a part of the psyche. He must necessarily escape observation, since he is the observer. Thus the standpoint from which commentary is made must always be one remove from experience, and cannot have attention focused upon it.

Our activity, then, comes before our reflection upon it, and reflection can tell us only what we have done, not what we are doing. The eye that is seeing cannot see itself.

There is a tendency at least implicit in the thinking of many psychotherapists to see conscious awareness as somehow 'higher' than the unconscious mental phenomena from whose influence they seek to free their patients. However, our discussion so far suggests that this may be putting the cart before the horse. This is a point made by Hayek in an interesting paper which he calls 'The Primacy of the Abstract'.[3] In this paper, Hayek puts forward the idea that our experience may be organized by what he calls 'action patterns'.

These are to be understood as kinds of templates which cannot in themselves be given to conscious awareness, but which determine, from 'above' as it were, what we actually experience:

It is generally taken for granted that in some sense conscious experience constitutes the 'highest' level in the hierarchy of mental events, and that what is not conscious has remained 'sub-conscious' because it has not yet risen to that level. There can of course be no doubt that many neural processes through which stimuli evoke actions do not become conscious because they proceed on literally too low a level of the central nervous system. But this is no justification for assuming that all the neural events determining action to which no distinct conscious experience corresponds are in this sense sub-conscious. If my conception is correct that abstract rules of which we are not aware determine the sensory (and other) 'qualities' which we consciously experience, this would mean that of much of what happens in our mind we are not aware, not because it proceeds at too low a level but because it proceeds at too high a level. It would seem more appropriate to call such processes not 'sub-conscious' but 'super-conscious', because they govern the conscious processes without appearing in them. This would mean that what we consciously experience is only a part, or the result, of processes of which we cannot be conscious, because it is only the multiple classification by the super-structure which assigns to a particular event that determined place in a comprehensive order which makes it a conscious event.

And:

The point in all this which I find most difficult to bring out clearly is that the formation of a new abstraction seems *never* to be the outcome of a conscious process, not something at which the mind can deliberately aim, but always a discovery of something which *already* guides its operation. This is closely connected with the fact that the capacity for abstraction manifests itself already in the actions of organisms to which we surely have no reason to attribute anything like consciousness, and that our own actions certainly provide ample evidence of being governed by abstract rules of which we are not aware.

The human being's most developed activity, therefore, is always 'out in front' of what he can say about himself. As we noted in the previous chapter, we tend to think of characteristically human behaviour, in the loftiest sense of the term, as being the result of some kind of conscious deliberation. What we find, however, is that such deliberation is in truth frequently more an account we give *after* the event. Not, of course, that we cannot do things deliberately. But what we do deliberately is done in the context of projects which we cannot know beforehand, though we may discover them as we go along.

There is, then, on the face of it nothing particularly unusual in the neurotic's inability to say what he is doing, nor is there necessarily anything ominously pathological about his failure to give an accurate account of his actions. What is interesting is the *use* which it seems can be made in neurosis of the phenomena we have been considering.

In his account of bad faith, Sartre gives an excellent example of the kind of use an individual might find for it:

... A homosexual has an intolerable feeling of guilt, and his whole existence is determined in relation to this feeling. One will readily foresee that he is in bad faith. In fact it frequently happens that this man, while recognizing his homosexual inclination, while avowing each and every particular misdeed which he has committed, refuses with all his strength to consider himself '*a paederast*'. His case is always 'different', peculiar; there enters into it something of a game, of chance, of bad luck; the mistakes are all in the past; they are explained by a certain conception of the beautiful which women can not satisfy; we should see in them the results of a restless search, rather than the manifestations of a deeply rooted tendency, etc., etc. Here is assuredly a man in bad faith who borders on the comic since, acknowledging all the facts which are imputed to him, he refuses to draw the conclusion which they impose. . . .

The homosexual recognizes his faults, but he struggles with all his strength against the crushing view that his mistakes constitute for him *a destiny*. He does not wish to let himself be considered a thing. He has an obscure but strong feeling that an homosexual is not an homosexual as this table is a table or as this red-haired man is red-haired. It seems to him that he has escaped from each mistake as soon as he has posited it and recognized it; he even feels that the psychic duration by itself cleanses him from each misdeed, constitutes for him an undetermined future, causes him to be born anew. Is he wrong? Does he not recognize in himself the peculiar, irreducible character of human reality? His attitude includes then an undeniable comprehension of truth. But at the same time he needs this perpetual rebirth, this constant escape in order to live; he must constantly put himself beyond reach in order to avoid the terrible judgment of collectivity. Thus he plays on the word *being*. He would be right actually if he understood the phrase, 'I am not a paederast' in the sense of 'I am not what I am'. That is, if he declared to himself, 'To the extent that a pattern of conduct is defined as the conduct of a paederast and to the extent that I have adopted this conduct, I am a paederast. But to the extent that human reality can not be finally defined by patterns of conduct, I am not one.' But instead he slides surreptitiously towards a different connotation of the word 'being'. He understands 'not being' in the sense of 'not-being-in-itself'. He lays claim to 'not being a paederast' in the sense in which this table *is not* an inkwell. He is in bad faith.[4]

What seems to distinguish neurotic 'bad faith', 'repression', or self-deception from a *natural* disjunction between words and actions (what one describes oneself as doing in contrast to what one actually does) is, then, its apparent purposefulness. In the normal run of events there are actions which *cannot* be accessible to reflective awareness or which cannot easily be put into words; on the other hand, in the case of neurotic self-deception, the person seems to be involved in an attempt to *prevent* his actions being put into words— he seems to be concerned to keep the significance of certain of his actions out of his awareness although he could do otherwise.

As has been pointed out, our most fundamental strategies, or, in Sartre's terminology, projects, are, at the time we are carrying them out, unknowable by us—though they may be apparent enough to somebody else. We may, again, be engaged in activities (like riding a bicycle, for example) the mechanics of which are hard to specify (you cannot *tell* someone how to ride a bicycle) although we are aware that we are carrying them out. Nevertheless, in pursuit of our projects, we may also at times call upon a repertoire of well-practised skills the nature of which is reflectively clear to us and which we can turn on or off at will. If we put these into action unthinkingly— habitually perhaps—we are, by reflecting for a moment, easily able to 'read off' their meaning: we can see what we're up to. The striking thing about the neurotic is that he seems to be engaged in relatively low-level strategic activities of this kind, the meaning of which seems clear to us, but which he seems to experience as unspecifiable— either he cannot say what he is doing (e.g. protecting himself from social encounters by means of symptoms) or is unable to criticize his own performance (e.g. cannot see that his social manner is unusually submissive). In other words he seems to treat his own behaviour *as if* it was of the kind we might accept as unspecifiable, although to others it looks rather like the kind of practised skill which we normally expect to be available to conscious awareness. What may make us particularly suspicious is that his concern that 'something is the matter' with him betrays a certain kind of awareness, a certain ability to evaluate his performance which, however, stops short of recognizing the obvious implications. This may be what distinguishes the neurotic from the eccentric—the latter simply gets on with his unusual activities, appearing to be 'lost' in them, while the former somehow stands outside his activities, and yet is unable to criticize them in the way which 'standing outside' would seem to permit.

In a penetrating study of the problem we are considering, Fingarette[5] describes the kind of neurotic strategy we are concerned with as a failure of the individual to 'spell out' his or her engagements or activities in particular cases:

> This is the situation in which there is overriding reason *not* to spell-out some engagement, where we skilfully take account of this and systematically avoid spelling-out the engagement, and where, in turn, we refrain from spelling-out this exercise of our skill in not spelling-out. In other words, we avoid becoming explicitly conscious of our engagement, and we avoid becoming explicitly conscious that we are avoiding it.

The question which immediately arises, naturally enough, is that of *how* someone achieves an intention not to spell out their engagements (and not to spell out that they are not spelling them out). To some extent, the ground has already been prepared for such an understanding, since it was established in the previous chapter that there is nothing unusual in people having intentions of which they are not aware. What we have to indicate specifically, then, is how somebody can not be aware of severing his activity from his reflective consciousness *intentionally*.

Sartre suggests that this can be achieved on an analogy with going to sleep:

> Let us understand clearly that there is no question of a reflective, voluntary decision, but of a spontaneous determination of our being. One *puts oneself* in bad faith as one goes to sleep and one is in bad faith as one dreams. Once this mode of being has been realized, it is as difficult to get out of it as to wake oneself up; bad faith is a type of being in the world, like waking or dreaming, which by itself tends to perpetuate itself. . . [6]

It is, of course, not easy to go to sleep on purpose. Sleep, as Fingarette suggests in his book, is something that happens to one rather than something one can make happen. And yet, I think, Sartre's analogy is an instructive one, since 'going to sleep' represents a special kind of alliance between what one can control and what one cannot. We learn the conditions which are conducive to sleep, and we take advantage of them; we put ourselves in the position in which sleep is likely to overtake us when the conditions are right (i.e. we go to bed, switch the light off, shut our eyes, etc.). In the same sort of way, the neurotic strategist puts himself in the position most suitable for remaining ignorant of what he is 'up to', and then allows, as it were, nature to take its course.

If the psychotherapist consults his own experience of his patients' self-deception, he will surely find clear instances of the kind of process under discussion. Indeed, the psychotherapeutic situation is one of the few in which neurotic self-deception can be observed closely—and indeed challenged—as it takes place. If the neurotic's task is one of misrepresenting to himself the significance of his strategies (for fear of what they will reveal to him), the presence of the therapist means that he has the additional problem of maintaining self-deception in the face of a critical consciousness (that of the therapist) which is *not* in an unspoken alliance with him; not only does he have to avoid his own critical scrutiny, but he also has to develop ways of avoiding the therapist's. Here, of course, we are back with the concept of resistance which was discussed in the previous chapter.

It is not difficult for the patient to misrepresent to the therapist (and himself) activity which has taken place outside the therapeutic situation, for in this case he can make use of straightforward 'bad faith'—he can confuse what he does with what he 'means' to do, or with what he 'thinks' he is doing. His behaviour within the therapeutic situation is not so easy to disguise, because, as has been said, he is under the critical gaze of the therapist. He can achieve his aim of non-recognition of what he is doing only by *not looking* at it, or by *distracting* his own attention when asked to look, or by steadfastly looking *somewhere else*.

Most therapists will, perhaps, be familiar with the way a person can 'not look' when his attention is drawn to what he is doing: he may suddenly become vague, in an odd way defocused, his eyes may literally become slightly glazed, his attention somehow scattered and imprecise, his thinking blunt and jumbled. In my own experience this kind of defocusing is the most striking, and perhaps the most common, method of maintaining self-deception in therapy.

The distraction of the person's attention from recognition of his strategies seems often to be achieved by means of symptoms, and it is to symptoms also that the patient may look when he wishes simply to divert his gaze from the direction indicated by the therapist to a (for him) less problematic area. On the whole these seem to be somewhat lower-level tactics than that of defocusing, and they are also, perhaps, from the patient's point of view, less successful. In the case of distraction, a patient may indulge directly in some kind of symptomatic behaviour—possibly but not necessarily connected with an obsession or phobia—in order to draw his own, and if possible also the therapist's attention away from his deeper projects. In the second case he may just stubbornly insist that it is his symptomatology, and not he, which is the problem. If these methods of maintaining self-deception are less successful than 'defocusing', it is largely because they are more obvious, more easily pointed out by the therapist, and almost impossible after a time not to recognize. Indeed, those patients who drop out of psychotherapy relatively quickly often seem to do so because their heavy reliance on either or both of these methods of maintaining self-deception is beginning to be eroded, and they are left with no alternative either to recognizing what they are doing or to leaving the situation altogether. Defocusing, however, is a much more subtle tactic: precisely at the point at which it is most obvious (to the therapist) it is also most difficult to see (for the patient).

There are a number of points about this account which it is important to understand. In the first place, I do not wish to suggest that in all cases the therapist is in a position to see better than the patient what the latter is 'really' doing. He does not establish the 'real' reasons for the patient's behaviour on the basis of some kind of expert appraisal, and simply tell him of his findings. If he is struck by the contrast between the patient's avowed intentions and his actual activity, his task is to *negotiate* with him a view of his behaviour which may account more satisfactorily for the incongruities observed. Because people are not static entities, there can be no 'correct' view of what they are or final version of what they are doing. For this reason, patient and therapist have to come to an agreement about what is happening which seems a useful basis for further exploration. If he is guided by this principle of negotiation (about which more will be said in the next chapter), rather than by any notion of technical mastery of the situation, the therapist will have little cause to be worried about the 'accuracy' of his statements to the patient; the latter will determine the pace of their relationship as well as the degree to which he accepts the therapist's influence, and is unlikely to take the therapist's utterances, whether accurate or mistaken, at their face value. Therapists who get worried about whether they have said the 'right thing' frequently operate in a context in which they feel they ought to be omniscient, if not omnipotent.

A further point I wish to make is that, although much of the therapist's time may be taken up in attempting to agree with the patient an alternative view of what he is 'up to', and consequently in fostering in him an awareness which formerly he did not possess, the *ultimate* aim of therapy cannot be to make people 'aware'. Awareness of self-deceptive strategies is a means of achieving mastery over certain aspects of one's behaviour, not an end in itself. For, as we have seen, the totally conscious person is an impossibility.

It is at least arguable that psychology and psychotherapy have traditionally concentrated too one-sidedly on conscious awareness as an ideal of human nature. It may not, for example, entirely be a caricature of psychoanalysis to represent it as contrasting 'healthy', conscious behaviour with the sexually and aggressively charged impulses of our unconscious minds, and this would suggest that most of our actions which are not the product of, or immediately accessible to, our reflective awareness are likely to be, as it were, tainted with *id*. As far as it accounts for our pre-reflective activity by reference to the unconscious, psychoanalysis carries with it, therefore, inescapable moral overtones: there is something slightly deplorable—almost even depraved—about the man whose actions are not bathed in the light of consciousness.

Many of the more modern psychotherapeutic techniques also tend to carry with them an implication that 'knowing yourself' is the most important aim to which you can aspire. George Kelly's 'repertory grid technique',[7] for example, provides one way in which a person can become aware of the ways in which he is interpreting ('construing') the actions of others, and the assumptions he is making about them. Briefly, the technique depends upon the patient specifying in what way any two people known to him are alike, and different from a third. This procedure can, of course, be carried out for an indefinite number of 'triads' of the patient's acquaintances, and is aimed at revealing to him the 'personal constructs' by means of which he orders his interpersonal world. Again, Kelly suggests that a person may learn a good deal about himself by writing a sympathetic autobiographical sketch of his life up to the moment of inquiry. It is probably true that the limitations of these techniques were clear enough to Kelly himself, but the use to which they are frequently put by some of those therapists who have been influenced by his writing seems often to fail to recognize that they cannot tell the person 'what he is like'. For reasons which have already been elaborated, the person somehow slips away from the light of his own inquiry, even when he is earnestly trying not to; he is inevitably in important ways different from what he says he is.

It seems, then, that if psychotherapy is characterized as a procedure for achieving self-awareness in any complete sense, it must be doomed to failure. Much of our most intricate and rich experience, many of our most complex skills, perhaps the majority of the rules which guide our action in day-to-day life, the very process of abstraction itself, may all, it seems, be out of reach of reflection. And if we succeed in pinning down and defining an aspect of our experience, or a strategy hitherto unrecognized, in the very process of doing so we become anchored in a standpoint which is itself unanalysable—we are being guided, in the terms used by Hayek, by new action patterns, or, in Sartre's, by new projects which are inaccessible to reflection. In so far as psychotherapy is aimed at self-awareness, then, it stands in danger of becoming an exercise in bad faith, and in so far as we try, as psychotherapists, to congeal our patients into a state of being 'understood' we are, to put it dramatically, denying them the very essence of their human nature. Whatever we are, we are not what we suppose ourselves to be or declare ourselves to be, and directly we *know* what we are (rather than what we were), we have fallen into self-deception.

However, there are some conclusions we should be careful *not* to draw from these considerations. I repeat that it is not my intention to suggest that self-critical reflection is a waste of time; that people are in all circumstances incapable of acting under the guidance of reflection; that therapy should be nothing but a prolonged indulgence in raw experience and wordless action.

If, however, as was concluded in the last chapter, people are free, and if the foundation of their being is unknowable in the sense we commonly use that word, then it would seem mistaken for psychotherapy to aim at any particular kind of frozen ideal of what people should be (for example, socially, sexually or vocationally 'adequate'; able to achieve 'heightened awareness' of themselves or others; well-rounded; outgoing; being at one with their physical bodies; free of 'unrealistic' fears; able to achieve 'peak experiences' with satisfactory frequency; able to be socially assertive; and so on and on). As *ends*, these aims are unsatisfactory if for no other reason than that, having achieved them, the person is still left going somewhere, and it would be unfortunate if he was led to feel that, for the sake of his 'mental health', he should know the name of his destination.

But if psychotherapy cannot set (*final*) positive and concrete aims for its patients, it can nevertheless make its intentions clear in a somewhat more abstract manner: that is, psychotherapy can be a procedure which helps people to clarify their misconceptions about themselves, and to accept that they are free to go where their actions, projects and strategies are taking them. Neurotic self-deception seems often to rest on the misconceptions which patients have about themselves, and human nature in general (for example, that anger is not permissible, that 'nice' mothers never feel irritation or rage with their babies, and so on), and which they maintain with great tenacity. At the centre of their misconceptions, often, is the *finality* which they perceive in them—they find themselves petrified, as it were, in a form which they experience as unbearable or unaccept-able. For the therapist to offer them another, if different, final state to aim at is simply to supplant one neurotic solution with another, and is equally misconceived. It is, then, not the therapist's business to peddle miniature Utopias for individuals to inhabit, but, by negotiating with the patient a new view of his predicament, to help him free himself from his immobility and send him on his way.

An important part, but only a part, of the therapeutic process of negotiation, will be for the therapist to help the patient to an awareness of some of the strategies which he is using in the service of self-deception. In this context, the kinds of techniques advocated by Kelly, and others, may play an important role. There are of course several technical procedures which rely heavily on reflective awareness and which help to clarify to the patient, before his very eyes so to speak, the nature of some of his strategies (though, once the game is up, they will be replaced by *new* strategies which will in turn *not* be available to his awareness, until again substituted by new ones, and so on). An exercise developed by Mair,[8] and based on what he calls a 'conversational model' of psychological relations, is a good example of such a procedure. In this, one person writes a character analysis of another which he is prepared to show him and discuss with him, and a further analysis which, initially at least, he is not prepared to show him, though as both parties gain confidence in the relationship they may reveal views which they were at first anxious to conceal. The insights which both parties may gain from this procedure (some of them, certainly, not easy to put into words) will be clear to anybody willing to try the experiment.

There are also, of course, many other techniques aimed at the clarification of interpersonal strategies, etc., but the point at issue here is that their value will depend on the context in which they are used: for example, is the patient supposed to discover only what the therapist thinks he should, or may he draw any conclusions he likes? Is he being moved from 'neurotic' position A to 'healthy' position B, or is he, so to speak, getting help in freeing his propeller from weeds so that he can go where he wants?

It is in fact precisely in 'freeing' people that reflective psychotherapeutic approaches can be most useful. Too often, however,
reflective procedures (like psychoanalytic interpretation, etc.) are
seen as bringing about *understanding* and self-knowledge of a kind
which enables the person thenceforth to carry around with him an
enriched version of himself from which he can, as it were, read off
suitable responses at appropriate moments; choosing, in a controlled
sort of way, actions to fit his circumstances in the bright light of full
consciousness. Far from freeing the person, however, this is freezing
him into the mould of what he currently accepts about himself.

With these arguments in mind, I think it possible to advance an
alternative view of reflection and a rather different purpose for the
kind of negotiating procedure which the psychoanalysts call
'interpretation'. *The point of understanding what you are doing now
is to enable you to do something else.* This is exactly the point of
interpreting neurotic behaviour—by seeing what his current projects
are the patient is able to undertake new ones, not simply to add to
his repertoire of conscious actions, or, more negatively, to stop doing
what he was doing before.

Self-consciousness tends often to disrupt or explode what it
reflects upon. Whether riding a bicycle or reading a book or talking
to friends, if you become self-consciously aware of what you are
doing you may well cease to do it effectively. 'Understanding', then,
becomes a way of exploding the person's current projects and
strategies, making them historical, and leaving him free to follow
new ones. Paradoxically, then, the use of techniques for promoting
self-consciousness in psychotherapy should be aimed at, and have
the inevitable result of, allowing the person to become unself-
conscious again.

Frankl's technique (already referred to in Chapter 2) of
'paradoxical intention', for example, makes good use of this
principle: patients who find themselves doing things they don't want
to do (e.g. stuttering) are asked to do them *on purpose*, and,
according to Frankl, frequently find themselves unable then to
produce the unwanted actions. A similar approach has been used in
psychotherapy with families as well as individuals by a group of
American therapists[9] who suggest to patients, again paradoxically,
that they carry out with conscious deliberation interpersonal
strategies which up to that point they had been practising unawares.

The, perhaps often unspoken, psychotherapeutic ideal of the fully
conscious person, performing his life with admirable virtuosity as,
with his inner eye, he reads from the richly orchestrated score his

self-knowledge has revealed, has, when one comes to think about it, something rather sickening about it. For it is impossible to act self-consciously and in good faith; the most successfully 'self-conscious' people of our time are probably confidence tricksters and television compères. Where reflection gives us control over our behaviour it does so at the expense of its spontaneity and its honesty—the latter because we cannot in truth *help* being spontaneous, and to do something self-consciously is to hide from view our spontaneity, to conceal our real, unself-conscious intention.

It is a common observation in social psychology that people may become conscious of themselves only because they can be objects of the consciousness of others: you learn about yourself through the eyes of others. Just as the other's consciousness of you turns you into an object, so your self-consciousness turns you into an object for yourself. Frequently this is a disrupting experience, a 'project-exploding' situation from which you struggle to break free to a realm of unobjectified activity. Neurotic patients frequently describe experiences (surely not entirely unfamiliar to the rest of us) which seem to centre on this kind of fear of being 'objectified' by others—so much so that a patient may feel, for example, that he cannot function properly in public places; he feels frozen with fear, his facial muscles refuse to form the expression he strives for, he is unable to eat in restaurants under the gaze of others, and so on. On the other hand, the confidence trickster, the orator, those television performers whose whole aim is *not* to appear to be performing (pundits and 'personalities') try deliberately to arrange their activity to conform to the objectification which is imposed upon them by the viewers. Their conscious manipulation of the situation means, however, that they are necessarily dishonest as far as their self-presentation is concerned; their being is concealed—unless for example, through a producer's error, they are revealed by the camera in an unguarded moment.

The phenomena of self-consciousness have fascinated psychologists to an extent where many have become more concerned with the deliberate manipulation of appearances than with man's capacity to act as a spontaneous agent. An analysis of 'non-verbal communication', for example, in which it is noted that a person's gestures and facial expressions may be interpreted by others as signifying something about that person, may be used to train people deliberately to emit non-verbal cues designed to convey a particular message. This, obviously, is precisely the art of the con-man—he looks and behaves like a retired British army colonel, with all that

that implies, though he is really an ex-convict in illicit pursuit of other people's money. The line between therapy and deceit is thus a very thin and delicate one. It is one thing to suggest to a person that he is conveying a certain impression of himself which conflicts with his actual intentions and so gets him into difficulties. It is quite another to suggest to him *how* to convey impressions which will conform to approved social expectations. The impression one gives, in other words, must, to be genuine, be linked to one's (ultimately) unself-conscious intention, not to certain concealed manipulative aims. Analyses such as those of Goffman[10] of the ways in which appearances influence social intercourse, penetrating though they are, stand in danger of developing if we are not careful into a psychological technology of deceit.

The aim of reflection and interpretation (negotiation) in psychotherapy, then, should be to free the individual from one project or set of strategies so that he can adopt new ones. Far from advancing an ideal of self-knowledge, we should in fact be using it as a means to an end—an end to which it is in fact paradoxically opposed. Instead, it might be (and often is) helpful to encourage patients to *trust* their non-reflective, unself-conscious activity, since the ultimate aim of psychotherapy can only be to enable the person to set off down paths he does not already know. Similarly, the therapist must at times trust himself to act unself-consciously within the therapeutic situation, and it is perhaps one of the greatest difficulties in conceptualizing and communicating about psychotherapy that so much of importance happens, when it happens, beyond the reach of reflection. Far from this being shamefully unscientific, it is inevitable that psychotherapy should have its tacit, unspecifiable aspects which can in no way be engineered before the therapeutic event, so to speak, and can only be characterized after the event, when they have become history. On the whole therapists do not yet seem to have come to terms with this satisfactorily, and beginning therapists are often ill-prepared to accept and exercise tacit skills and unrehearsed activity without feeling that they have departed disastrously from some kind of therapist's handbook, and entered regions which are reprehensibly unprofessional.

1 Freud, S. (1915). *Standard Edition of the Complete Psychological Works*. Trans. and ed. James Strachey. Vol. XIV, p. 201. London: Hogarth.
2 Harré, R. and Secord, P. F. (1972). *The Explanation of Social Behaviour*. Oxford: Blackwell.

3 Hayek, F. A. (1972). The primacy of the abstract. In A. Koestler and J. R. Smythies (eds.). *Beyond Reductionism*. London: Hutchinson.

4 Sartre, J.-P. (1969). *Being and Nothingness*. Trans. H. E. Barnes. p. 63. London: Methuen. Reprinted by permission of Philosophical Library, Inc. Copyright © 1956 by Philosophical Library, Inc.

5 Fingarette, H. (1969). *Self-Deception*. London: Routledge & Kegan Paul.

6 op. cit., p. 68.

7 Kelly, G. A. (1955). *The Psychology of Personal Constructs*. Vol. 1. New York: Norton.

8 Mair, J. M. M. (1970). Experimenting with individuals. *British Journal of Medical Psychology*, **43**, 245.

9 See for example P. Watzlawick, J. H. Weakland and R. Fisch. (1974). *Change*. New York: Norton, and J. Haley. (1963). *Strategies of Psychotherapy*. New York: Grune & Stratton.

10 Goffman, E. (1971). *The Presentation of Self in Everyday Life*. Harmondsworth: Penguin Books.

7

Aspects of Negotiation

Although it is often referred to as such, psychotherapy is obviously not a 'talking cure'. Apart from affording temporary feelings of relief at having 'got things off one's chest', talking on its own does not seem to be a particularly fruitful way of dealing with one's problems. Nobody solves problems simply by juggling them in his head. Psychotherapy, then, is not just an armchair debate between two (or more) people, but an active relationship which has implications reaching out beyond the therapeutic setting. The patient does more than talk: he acts and experiences.

Nevertheless, for most forms of psychotherapy, talking is what therapists and patients seem to be doing most of the time, and verbal communication provides the vehicle for much of what happens in the therapeutic situation. Unimportant in itself, talking, therefore, seems to serve some important therapeutic ends.

It would not be possible in any book on psychotherapy to provide exhaustive coverage of all the things that can happen during the course of therapy; it may be that a therapeutic result could be brought about by entirely unexpected and unique sets of circumstances which could in no way be legislated for in advance. On the other hand, some processes occur with such regularity that they seem almost inevitable. The process of negotiation—a concept already used several times in earlier chapters—is one of the most outstanding of the regular features of therapy, and constitutes one of the main reasons for talking.

Before the patient can do anything about his problems, he has to negotiate with the therapist a view of them about which both can agree; successful therapeutic work proceeds, at least in part, on the ground of experience which is shared between patient and therapist. Each has to know, in other words, what the other is talking about.

As we have already seen, it is no simple matter for a person to know what he himself is talking about, let alone someone else. Except in some very basic areas of our experience, largely confined to our relations with the physical world, it is not obvious that we share a common view to any great extent: the meanings we attach to people, ideas and relationships are largely individual, even though our vocabulary often gives them a misleading appearance of objective identity. Moreover, even when we have our own meanings clearly in sight, they are liable to shift and change with new experiences. There is, therefore, no objective 'truth' about people which can be known; there is an indeterminate number of perspectives on any person, including his own, some of which may be more stable than others, but none of which can be said to be either fundamental or permanent. What a person 'is', or is doing at any point in his development, is therefore a matter of negotiation between interested perspectives. In psychotherapy, these are the perspectives of the patient on the one hand and the therapist on the other.

There seem to me to be two main elements of negotiation: under-standing, and persuasion. Clearly, if you are to find out what another person is talking about, it is important that you understand him; and if the significance of what he is saying eludes you at first, he may have to persuade you of its relevance. Again, if the therapist is to influence or encourage the patient to change, he may well find that merely understanding him is not enough—he may have to persuade him that alternative views of his predicament are possible.

On the whole the psychotherapy literature has concentrated on understanding far more than on persuasion (to conceptualize both as parts of a process of negotiation is rare in psychotherapy[1]). The way in which the therapist may be said to 'understand' his patient has undergone a fairly radical change, theoretically speaking, over the years, and we shall consider this development shortly. That persuasion has not featured greatly in psychotherapeutic thinking until relatively recently may well reflect a certain nervousness psychotherapists feel about being exposed to accusations of 'influencing' people. It was at one time common for therapists to contrast the neutral freedom of 'psychological' therapies with the distasteful manipulativeness of behavioural methods. In the former case the therapist preserved his neutral mask, scrupulously avoiding imposing his personality upon the patient, for fear of using him for his own 'pathological ends', while the behaviour therapist, it was felt, surreptitiously manipulated the stimuli which would, according to his theory, determine the appropriate responses. Either type of therapist could, in fact, feel superior about the other: the psychotherapist could accuse the behaviour therapist of making damaging use of his powers, while the latter could sneer at the former for ignoring the fact that he is a determining stimulus in the patient's environment whether he likes it or not. Both these approaches, however, make the error of characterizing human relationships as *determining*. The behaviour therapist proclaims the error boldly, and so fails to see that his patients do not *have* to follow his influence; the psychotherapist implies a mistakenly deterministic view by trying so hard to *avoid* determining his patient's reactions. The result is that he fails to make rational use of the influence which is open to him.

As we have seen, patients' actions are not determined by their therapists, and therapists are not responsible for what patients do. The therapist's attempts to persuade his patients of the cogency of his perspective, or the usefulness of a certain possible course of action, may or may not be successful, and what the patient decides to do in the end is his responsibility. Nevertheless, the degree to which the therapist is able to influence the patient may be a crucial factor in the latter's arriving at a new perspective or setting out on a new course of action. This influence is, in the last analysis, an intensely personal matter, and one which the therapist must come to terms with, however much he might prefer to hide behind the guise of professional expert, impersonally applying a mechanical technique. How effective an influence he is will depend in part upon the extent of the basis of common understanding the therapist is able to establish with his patient.

In more orthodox psychoanalytic psychotherapy, 'understanding' was, perhaps, often seen as a largely one-way affair in which the therapist could understand the patient better than the patient could understand himself, largely because the therapist had access to the mysteries of the Unconscious and the patient did not. One of the tasks of therapy in this kind of situation was, then, for the patient to come to understand himself in the same terms as those used by his therapist. 'Interpretation' was, largely, the vehicle by means of which the patient was to be persuaded of the validity of the analyst's perspective.

In many ways, of course, this follows the technical model of medicine: the doctor knows what is good for the patient, and the patient gets better when he comes to accept and act upon the doctor's view. In psychiatry, certainly, it is this model which is used to determine the 'sanity' of the patient's perspective: in traditional psychiatric diagnosis it is not *what* the patient tells his doctor which is important so much as *how* he tells it. Is he slow ('retarded'), is his speech articulate and his logic clear, does he describe things in a way which makes conventionally good sense, and so on? The actual, 'interior' significance of what the patient *means* is of no interest to the psychiatrist, who is looking simply for symptoms and signs of 'illness'. The patient will be judged 'better' when the symptoms and signs have vanished, i.e. when the form of his communications is again in line with what is conventionally acceptable. Similarly, the psychoanalyst will be listening to the patient's free associations not for their surface meaning, but for indications of unconscious pathology according with Freud's formulations. The patient's ability to accept the analyst's interpretations of what he is actually saying for what he is 'really' (unconsciously) meaning, will be an indication of his improvement. In a nutshell, understanding in this sense consists in the therapist's reinterpretation of the patient's communications into a form which fits the former's theoretical framework, and this process is achieved with the help of some kind of technical lexicon. In recent decades this kind of approach to understanding has been radically challenged, and to a large extent replaced, by its polar opposite.

In psychotherapy, the writings of such theorists as Rogers and Kelly have led to a widespread acceptance among therapists generally of a view of understanding as 'empathy'. Rogers in particular stresses the therapeutic importance of the therapist's understanding the patient *from the patient's perspective*. In order to grasp the meaning *for him* of the patient's experience, the therapist has to put himself in the patient's shoes, to try his level best to see the world from where the patient sees it. Rather than the patient having to learn the therapist's language and theoretical system, the therapist has to learn the patient's. In this, he has to attend not so much to the patient's words, as to their meaning for the patient.

As we have already noted, Rogers considers this kind of empathy to be one of the essential conditions for therapeutic change (the other two being warmth and genuineness). Kelly also makes the relativity of perspectives central to his psychology—to understand what another person is doing entails an understanding of the unique organization of his 'personal constructs', and such an understanding can only be gleaned through painstaking inquiry with the person himself. To attempt, as psychologists often do, to explain others by 'measuring' them with questionnaires of introversion-extraversion, neuroticism, etc., is one-sidedly to impose upon them the *psychologist's* way of looking at the world. But people act on the basis of *their* conceptions, not those of the psychologist, and their actions cannot be understood in any other context.

In a rather similar vein, R. D. Laing[2] has striven to shift the attention of British psychiatrists from the formal conventionality of what patients say to the meaning *for them* of their communications. 'Psychotic symptoms', Laing suggests, may be the understandable, perhaps inevitable, result of patients' experience, rather than mere indications of disease pathology; 'psychosis' thus becomes a way of dealing with an 'unlivable situation' rather than a 'mental disease', a way which may, moreover, be *understood* by the psychiatrist who is willing carefully to investigate with the patient the significance of his experience.

The more modern view of 'empathy', particularly as expounded by Rogers, gave impetus to strategies of research into the accurate understanding of one person by another which had been a focus of interest in academic social psychology for some time. Much of this research, as pointed out in an earlier chapter, has a curiously mechanistic bias, and rests on the assumption that 'understanding others', is something like a *skill*, which some people are liable to have relatively more of than others. In the therapeutic situation, this becomes extended to the view that some therapists will be more empathetic than others, and that those who 'have it' will, following Rogers' views, be more therapeutically effective than those who do not. As we saw, there is a degree of evidence for this latter view, though it seems to depend more on how patients *see* their therapists than on an objective demonstration that some therapists 'possess' empathy while others do not.

The bias towards conceptualizing empathy as a kind of skill which people either have or do not have is probably a reflection of psychology's pervasive concern with 'traits' rather than with processes. Psychologists interested in the broad area of personality have—naturally enough, perhaps, and sometimes with fruitful results—tended to concentrate on those aspects of people's personal functioning which seem to possess considerable stability. A person is recognizable as the *same* person from one day to the next, and this depends as much on the familiarity and stability of his personal style as on the constancy of his physical appearance. Part at least of our definition of sanity rests on there being a considerable degree of predictability in personal behaviour. These relatively stable aspects of personality ('traits'), apart from their obvious intrinsic interest, have also been of particular concern because they are relatively easily measurable. What more natural in this setting, then, than to consider 'empathy' as yet another instance of a trait? (And what more inevitable than that psychological research 'findings' about empathy should reflect the assumptions which are made about it at the outset?)

In fact, research findings in this area are, as so often in psychological research, equivocal, and to provide a detailed review here would make tedious reading. In general, the stability of empathy as a trait which somebody can express at different times and in different situations seems to depend very much on the method which psychologists use to measure it, and, because psychologists rarely use the same methods in their research, results are conflicting. The evidence for a stable trait of empathy is thus not strong, though there is some work[3] which suggests that some people may be consistently more accurate than others in judging what particular people are likely to do in particular situations.

Although a general, stable trait of empathy has not been convincingly demonstrated, there have been some interesting findings concerning the *sort* of people who have been found to have a measurable degree of accurate empathy in particular research studies. The interesting point about this research[4] is that people who are better able to make accurate judgments about others tend *not* to be people who have a particular psychological theory about 'what makes people tick'. Conventional professional psychologists have in this way been found on the whole to make less good judges than have intelligent laymen, especially where the latter are people of wide-ranging—perhaps artistic—interests. Although one in the eye for the professionals, this is scarcely a surprising finding. The majority of psychological theories are—some might say necessarily—simplified models of human behaviour, appealing as a rule to a handful of singularly uncomplicated mechanistic concepts. Though they may be of some use in marshalling the 'facts' of mass behaviour, they are unlikely to deal effectively with the complexities of the individual case, and it is small wonder that a reasonably intelligent and sensitive person is likely to make better guesses about others if he relies more on the skills he has spent his life developing than on the crudely insensitive conceptual equipment of traditional psychology.

The particular emphasis of this kind of research on empathy is, then, blatantly materialistic. Empathy becomes a kind of psychological possession which, in the therapeutic situation, therapists may possess to a greater or lesser extent. Since, as we have said, therapist empathy has been shown in some research studies (though the evidence is by no means consistent) to be related to positive therapeutic outcome, it therefore becomes important for therapists who have not 'got' empathy to acquire it through training—they may, for example, be instructed in the kind of therapeutic 'responses' which are judged by impartial observers to be empathetic. In this sort of procedure, the absurdity of psychological materialism is fully exposed, and in attempting to turn empathy into a technical skill, we have lost sight of its nature as a *process* of understanding; an active experience is substituted by an appearance. Having discovered that understanding is an important ingredient of psychotherapy, the technical therapist immediately becomes preoccupied with finding out how to *appear* to be understanding, overlooking the fact that understanding is an *interpersonal process*.

However, not all psychological research in this area has been quite as crass as I have so far suggested, and some consideration of further research findings might help to take our inquiry a step further.

Some of the earlier research studies in the area of 'person perception'—a concern in the field of social psychology closely related to the concept of empathy—noted[5] that accurate judgment of one person by another is facilitated by actual similarity in personality between those involved. In other words, I find it easier to understand you if you are already like me in the first place. This finding has also received support in more recent research studies.[6]

In many ways, this observation makes good sense, focusing as it does on the process by means of which understanding is achieved through shared experience. Curiously, though, some of the psychologists carrying out the earlier studies somehow felt understanding on the basis of similarity to be cheating. Possibly because they thought that empathy should be some kind of, perhaps rather esoteric, skill, they seemed to feel that a person does not deserve to be called empathetic if he achieves accurate understanding of another simply because he is himself a rather similar person. 'Putting yourself in somebody else's shoes' should be a more effortful and clever procedure. They were also worried about the possibility that good judges of others might just be using social stereotypes which result in accurate description more or less by accident.

More recently, however, psychologists have come to the realization that there is nothing illicit about this kind of understanding,[7] and indeed it may *only* be on the basis of shared experience that understanding, or even real communication, is possible. Even so, one can understand that some uneasiness should be occasioned by such a view. For example, simply by *assuming* that everyone is like yourself you are bound to be right some of the time purely by chance, and yet this process looks more like what Freud called 'projection' than like true understanding.

What makes the difference, perhaps, between empathy and projection is that with the latter there is no readiness to compromise in situations where experience does not happen to be shared (combined, possibly, with the assumption that if people do not react like oneself, then there must be something the matter with them). What distinguishes the empathetic person, therefore, may be, in cases where he does not happen to share the experience of another, a willingness to *learn* how the other has come to see things the way he does. Empathy (if it must be treated like a trait) then becomes a willingness to find out about others rather than an ability to make accurate judgments about them from the outset. The essential point, however, is that understanding itself can only be based upon a shared 'position', however this may ultimately be achieved.

There is little doubt that recent emphasis on the importance of empathy in psychotherapy, even if it has here and there been tinged with a degree of naïve psychological materialism, has done much to minimize the violence which therapists could wreak on their patients. For the therapist simply to undercut his patient's experience and attempt to replace the conclusions it has led to with views derived from his own theoretical posture seems at best arrogant and at worst dangerous. The worst effects of such an approach can be seen most clearly in traditional psychiatric institutions in which diagnosis and the physical treatment of 'illness' are the central concerns of those involved. Psychologically, patients in such institutions are simply neglected: they are not people with problems, but objects with diseases. Nobody bothers to find out who they are; they are merely observed for the signs and symptoms they may emit or cease to emit.

And yet, again, understanding on its own is not enough. There is no obvious reason why 'being understood' should lead to great therapeutic change, although it may help someone to get a more objective view of himself and to become aware of activity of which he was formerly not aware. Understanding is, however, the necessary prerequisite for negotiation. Therapist and patient must learn each other's language if they are to be susceptible to each other's influence. Therapeutic communication consists of persuasion as well as understanding, an effort to learn as well as a sharing.

In this respect, the therapeutic situation may be likened to that of master and apprentice. The apprentice learns the master's skills, comes to see, as it were, his point of view by exposing himself to the experiences which the master has been through. The master cannot teach him directly, but knows what position he should take up in order to find out for himself. Whether therapist or patient is master or apprentice will vary according to who is trying to learn what from whom; in the process of negotiation each may have to struggle to recast those elements of his experience which are not available to the other in terms of elements which the other does possess (or at least possesses partially), or deliberately to place himself in the position of the other to find out what follows from it.

Learning, understanding and communication take place in a context of lived experience, not in any abstract cerebral sphere. Things are *known* through the bodily relations one has with them, and having an abstract idea of principles is a long way from experiencing bodily what they were derived from. If the reader doubts this assertion, let him compare the theoretical 'knowledge' of changing a wheel on a car or a washer on a tap, or making an omelette, with the actuality of doing it. Who ever learned to play the piano by reading a treatise about it? This is well recognized in the acquisition of, and communication about, manual and artistic skills, but it is often overlooked by those who, like psychotherapists, tend to spend much of their education immersed in abstract ideas. And yet most students will recall a point at which what they had learned about in books suddenly 'came alive'—and underwent a radical change of meaning—when they confronted the problems in their embodied activity.

The psychotherapist who seeks to understand his patient's problems by mentally 'searching the literature' for similar cases and drawing abstract parallels is likely to go sadly astray. If he cannot find things *within his own lived experience* which match what his patient is telling him, he must resolve either to find out by becoming an apprentice, or to acknowledge his inability to say anything particularly helpful about it. Fortunately, therapists probably do share with their patients a knowledge of the kinds of distress which the latter complain of, far more than the 'pathologizing' influence of the illness model of psychiatry encourages them to admit. Who has not been afraid of what people think about them ('social anxiety'), superstitiously cautious and ritualistic ('obsessional'), suspicious of the opinions and intentions of others ('paranoid'), sexually unresponsive ('impotent', or 'frigid'), depressed ('depressed'), excited ('manic'), and so on and on? Any therapist who prefers a technical lexicon to his own experience rejects *sharing* with his patient for attempted manipulation of him, and runs the risk of cutting him off, perhaps cruelly, from the support he needs to pursue the therapeutic exploration further. What, indeed, may *make* the therapist a master worthy of an apprentice is precisely that he does share the patient's 'pathological' features, but is able to view them in a different light or use them in a different way. In this respect, it is of interest that comparison of the personalities of psychotherapists with those of psychiatrists inclined to physical treatment methods, in most research studies, reveals a greater amount of 'neuroticism' or 'psychopathology' amongst the former group.

That understanding may arise from the bodily sharing of similar experience is a principle made wide use of in some of the techniques used by 'growth' psychologists, in particular in the 'encounter group' movement. 'Group cohesion' may be quickly established by encouraging participants to take part in certain exercises—exploring each other by means of touch, gazing into each other's eyes, etc.—or members may be told to act out physically the emotions they are talking about, and so on. Frequently members of such groups find these and related experiences illuminating and rewarding. Sometimes, on the other hand, such 'encounters' seem to be tinged with a kind of evangelistic zeal which blunts the more critical, and self-critical, faculties of those taking part. This is perhaps particularly the case where such procedures are linked to some kind of 'growth' ideal about how people should be—e.g. that it's good to express emotions, essential to be in touch with your body, desirable that everybody should be warm and loving toward everybody else. In such cases, the pressure to conform to the social standards set by the group tends to sweep the participant beyond the point at which he can assimilate the effects of these 'experiential' procedures into his personal construction of the world, and, though he may find himself in a somewhat exalted and elated state for a few days, he is likely quickly to find himself back where he started. It is certainly part of the negotiating process for me to put myself in your position to see if I find what you found there; but I must still be free *not* to find what you found, and to negotiate the discrepancy with you. If you insist that I have *got* to find what you found, because you know what's *good* for people and I don't, the essential quality of negotiation is destroyed.

Understanding, learning, sharing and communicating are perhaps the inevitable goals of our negotiating with each other, and are central not only to psychotherapy, but to almost all human activities. But it might be unfortunate if we saw them as ends in themselves: if, for example, mutuality pure and simple came to be seen as 'the' therapeutic goal, or as the ideal form of human existence. There is no doubt that understanding and communication as pervasive characteristics of society would be welcome replacements for the kind of concealed tribalism and 'club membership' which characterize most modern social intercourse, but the question remains, what would they be for? What could we do with this warm mutuality, once we had got over the novelty of basking in it? When we negotiate, we are not negotiating simply in order to share, but to share *something*.

That 'something' seems to me to be very much to do with our individuality, the furthest reaches of our inarticulate activity, the unknowable vanguard of our projects. What we may *eventually* come to recognize through negotiating and sharing its validity with others, is inevitably born in isolation, and too much 'therapeutic' emphasis on the cosiness of empathetic mutuality (an emphasis which sometimes expresses itself in group psychotherapies as an intense hostility to individual activity) threatens to cut us off from the very source of our activity. The result is what Cooper [8] calls 'a sterile, "emptied-out" form of group existence'.

If, by insisting that everything the individual does must be understood or understandable, we fail to accord validity to his individuality, we are likely to poison his creativity with despair. As has been said before, the aim of psychotherapy must be to free the person actively to pursue his projects wherever they lead him, not simply to anchor him in some kind of safe social haven where he can feel at one with his fellows. Neurotic strategies tend themselves to be immobilizing: they protect the person from the risks involved in giving himself over to pure activity. But life is a risky business, and many of those risks have to be borne in isolation. However much we may hope eventually to share our personal discoveries with others, we have to make them alone by taking risks, and if we try to protect people from the isolation of risk-taking by understanding them, we either prevent them from making discoveries in the first place, or plunge them into despair when they find themselves alone.

What this means in practice is that *trust* should take over where understanding ceases. Where my experience no longer follows yours, where we have exhausted all possibility of finding or expanding areas of our experience which overlap, I can at least support you in your isolation by trusting your experience to be valid.

The master-therapist may recognize as familiar in his own

experience many of the strategies used by the apprentice-patient, and through painstaking negotiation may encourage him to gain the personal skills necessary to deal with his problems. But it is obviously both possible and beneficial that an apprentice may develop skills and directions for his activities different from or beyond those of his master, and where this happens, he should be trusted to get on with the job without interference.

1 This has, however, been done in the field of social psychology by Harré and Secord, whose book *The Explanation of Social Behaviour* has been referred to in the previous chapter.

2 See, for example, R. D. Laing. (1960). *The Divided Self.* London: Tavistock, and (1967) *The Politics of Experience and the Bird of Paradise.* Harmondsworth: Penguin Books.

3 e.g., R. E. Fancher. (1969). Group and individual accuracy in person perception. *Journal of Consulting and Clinical Psychology*, **33**, 127. This paper contains references to Fancher's earlier work, which is also relevant.

4 See the review article by R. Taft. (1955). The ability to judge people. *Psychological Bulletin*, **52**, 1. Fancher's work is also relevant in this respect.

5 Cronbach, L. J. (1955). Processes affecting scores on 'understanding of others' and 'assumed similarity'. *Psychological Bulletin*, **52**, 177. Also: A. H. Hastorf and I. E. Bender. (1952). A caution respecting the measurement of empathic ability. *Journal of Abnormal and Social Psychology*, **47**, 574.

6 See, for example, A. A. Adinolfi. (1971). Relevance of person perception research to clinical psychology. *Journal of Consulting and Clinical Psychology*, **37**, 167. Also: E. J. Phares and K. G. Wilson. (1971). Internal-external control, interpersonal attraction, and empathy. *Psychological Reports*, **28**, 543.

7 See the paper by Adinolfi referred to above, and L. Christensen. (1974). Generality of personality assessment. *Journal of Consulting and Clinical Psychology*, **42**, 59.

8 Cooper, D. (1967). *Psychiatry and Anti-Psychiatry*. London: Tavistock.

8

The Practice of Psychotherapy

In this final chapter I shall attempt to draw together some of the observations which have been made earlier in this book, and then proceed to a consideration of their significance for the professional practice of psychotherapy.

My wish is to present a sketch of the psychotherapeutic process largely free from traditional theoretical preconceptions—a sketch, that is, which takes the personal experience of both therapist and patient seriously. The best way of doing this I can think of is to suggest how the course of therapy might run for a novice therapist faced with a new patient. In no way do I want to suggest that what follows provides a model of psychotherapy: it is intended merely as a more or less arbitrary device for organizing the phenomena which have been considered in earlier chapters.

It is quite likely that the first thing to be experienced by our beginning therapist and his new patient will be an alarming confusion. The patient, finding, as it were, his symptoms under attack, finds also that they shift, change, disappear, re-emerge subtly altered, give way to preoccupations and fears the existence of which he had not before suspected. This is not the mere mechanical operation of 'symptom substitution', but a situation which arises when the *meaning* of 'symptoms' is challenged (even if only implicitly) by the therapist's scrutiny.

The therapist, correspondingly, may find that the tools, skills and techniques which he has learned about in theory seem in some strange way to have no real application; the patient does not react as he is supposed to, his symptoms are stubbornly unresponsive, or suddenly vanish for the wrong reason, and, what's more, without the patient seeming to care or be pleased. The therapist may find himself being drawn into ways of relating to his patient which were not discussed in the textbooks and which make him feel professionally uncomfortable—answering questions which he doesn't really know the answers to, trying to meet needs he hasn't even identified, finding himself engaged in lengthy interactions the content of which he simply doesn't recognize from his theoretical training; he may discover at the end of the therapeutic session that for an hour or more he has been acting without apparent purpose or direction and has no clue about what has actually taken place. His anxieties about this state of affairs may be greatly heightened by his patient asking him what 'the point' of it all is, or observing that therapy doesn't seem to have 'done him any good' yet.

Clearly enough, what both patient and therapist need in a situation such as this is some way of organizing it. As far as the therapist is concerned, this may be achieved by the resolute, if somewhat desperate, application of a theoretical model, and, in face of all the confusion, the patient may be grateful enough to have such a model imposed upon him. If no organization at all is achieved, either patient or therapist or both may take fright, conclude that the patient cannot be helped (is for some reason 'unsuitable' for the kind of treatment being proffered) and close off the therapeutic contact.

However, if the participants, in particular the therapist, are able to accept their experience with a measure of equanimity and examine it in good faith, a third option is open to them. And that is to explore the meaning *for them* of the predicament in which they find themselves, to look for a way of drawing out of their situation an organization which in a sense it already contains, which is unique to it, and which, between them, they have given it. So we see that the confusion of the earlier stages of therapy is alarming only if it is seen as not conforming to a state of affairs which *should* exist (from the patient's standpoint, according to his expectations; from the therapist's, according to his theory). If, on the other hand, the confusion is seen as the more or less inevitable result of two strangers trying to make sense of each other's experience and intentions, it may lose much of its threatening character, and the joint attempt to investigate and elaborate the meaning of their situation for the participants may then become the central focus of therapy.

The emphasis in the first half of therapy thus becomes one of clarification and negotiation. Before therapy can proceed, patient and therapist have to co-operate in reaching for a shared understanding of the nature of their enterprise, and indeed of the nature of the patient's problems.

The ground for the negotiation is formed by the different perspectives of therapist and patient on the latter's problems. Where the patient sees symptoms or immutable personality traits (self-descriptions) which cripple him and hold him back from social activity, etc., the therapist is likely to see strategic evasions by means of which the patient actively keeps himself from feared situations. The patient will see himself as sufferer, the therapist will see him as agent. While the therapist may attempt to 'explode' the patient's projects, and thus render him free of them, the patient will manoeuvre self-deceptively to remain unaware of them. It may perhaps be helpful to indicate some of the issues around which such negotiations can centre.

A particularly frequent circumstance is one in which a person will use his symptoms in a way which prevents face-to-face confrontation with aspects of his nature which, if he were to take them seriously, would inescapably lead him to the conclusion that he was basically bad, or basically worthless. Thus, for example, a woman whose view of the world simply excludes anger or aggression as a justifiable human response, suddenly finds herself 'blacking out' in situations where (from an external observer's viewpoint) anger would be appropriate. The therapeutic task in this case may be for the therapist to negotiate with her a new way of looking at the situations in which she faints. To her there seems to be no common element in these occasions. She does not see anger as an appropriate response to them because, for her, anger is not possible; it simply does not exist as an available reaction. She thus has to become the therapist's apprentice in learning how to be angry.

Again, deep and pervasive feelings of worthlessness may lead a person to take up a stance in the world as an invalid—suffering perhaps from a whole range of debilitating physical symptoms (dizziness, nausea, stomach pains, headaches). The symptoms are of course 'real'; they are the physical expression of anxiety, but they have become detached from the *meaning* of anxiety. Because the symptoms are 'there', it is possible for the patient to use them to withdraw from the world and yet still be a *person* in it, albeit a sick person. An invalid can be loved, even admired as one coping heroically with adversity, and can thus maintain an element of self-respect. Stripped of his illness, on the other hand, such a person is brought face to face with what appears to him as his incompetence, cowardice, uselessness, inability to gain a purchase on the world in the way 'real people' seem to, yawning emptiness in his relations with those around him. In this kind of situation (of which there are many variants, not all involving an 'invalid' role) the therapeutic negotiation tends to centre round the individual's (often inordinately high) standards of personhood: he may need to learn that weakness or fear do not disqualify one from being loved, that courageous action does not necessarily entail self-destruction, that he is not identical with those aspects of himself which he hates. It is on this kind of renegotiation of personal standards that the psychotherapeutic approach of Albert Ellis (see Chapter 2) seems to concentrate most heavily.

The question of *risk* is one which seems also frequently to arise in the course of therapeutic contact, as we have already briefly noted, and may again appear in a variety of guises. This may be expressed by patients themselves in some kind of metaphor—e.g. 'it's better not to enter a race at all than to enter it and lose'. In this sort of situation symptoms—as so often, puzzling and inexplicable from the patient's point of view—arise to lay the person low just when he or she appears to be coping successfully with life, perhaps following promotion at work or the establishment of a new and apparently promising relationship. Or possibly, as much to his own surprise as to that of those around him, the person finds himself turning down opportunities or leaving situations which he has long desired or for which he has worked hard. Here again there is unlikely to be any recognition—until, that is, the process of therapeutic negotiation is well under way—that any fear of failure is involved. Having achieved some kind of success, and therefore established a degree of self-respect, etc., such a person seems to become intensely threatened by the possibility of failing in the course of further exposure to the situation. So nothing is followed through, and, though he does not see it this way, the person himself brings about the result he most fears: he aborts failure, so to speak, but in doing so abandons success. This kind of control of intolerable anxiety in risk-taking is of course frequently under discussion in the therapeutic literature.[1]

There are of course also those for whom any kind of risk is inadmissible, and who for this reason do not even get as far as any initial success. Their lives may be overshadowed by a gloomy, fatalistic pessimism which may resemble an intense, perpetual, hovering depression. No project is worth embarking upon, no pleasure worth indulging, no joy worth reaching towards; for, once achieved, it will only be snatched away, leaving behind it nothing but dust and ashes. Since love must lead to bereavement, it is better not to love, but to remain resolutely behind the battlements, warding off any advances the world may make. In a particularly sensitive and insightful paper,[2] Scott and Ashworth have shown the effects that this kind of attitude can have on those around the individual who adopts it; how, for example, parents may 'close off' their feelings for a child for fear of what may happen if they continue to involve themselves with it. Presumably 'normal' pessimism is not dissimilar in intent, and is less an expression of an appetite for gloom than an attempt at rendering the world a less (unexpectedly) painful place. For the pessimist, there can only be nice surprises.

It is presumably most often the case that the person who avoids risking a continuous engagement in the world for fear of failure also recognizes that he does not *control* the world. For if he could *make* things go his way, the likelihood of failure would be greatly diminished. Rather, he sees the world in terms of himself versus an inexorable Fate. This leads us to a consideration of those people who make use of an alternative strategy, that of attaining mastery over the world's unpredictability. Perhaps the easiest way of controlling the complexity and the confusion of the events taking place around one, and hence the anxiety associated with the probability of unexpected demands being made, is to attempt to limit in some way the spatio-temporal dimensions of one's existence. Personal moral standards again dictate, of course, that this has to be done blamelessly, and so by factors outside the individual's control. Symptoms—perhaps of a phobic nature—can be particularly useful in limiting contact with the world, and keeping the person's activities confined within a relatively manageable sphere of operations. An 'agoraphobic', for example, may *be overcome* by fear when venturing forth into the world, but does not recognize that he or she *is afraid*. Indeed, he *wants* to go out, to go to parties, etc., as he used to. It is of course precisely here that the self-deceptive strategies discussed earlier play such a major role: the person uses his symptoms to solve, without conscious dishonesty, the problem of how to run away without being a coward. (Agoraphobia may of course have many meanings; such symptoms are discussed here for illustrative purposes, and there is no intention of suggesting that this is what agoraphobia is 'really' about.)

Again, a person may simplify the world, and thus make it more controllable, by simplifying the ways in which he construes it. Thus his judgments about those around him may rest on a rigid, narrow, black-or-white moralism which enables him comfortably to categorize any event or relationship which might otherwise take him by surprise. Or, alternatively, the world may be simplified in its social structure (people who are for me versus people who are against me), or some other crude and all-embracing principle. Kelly's psychology of personal constructs is particularly helpful in understanding the structural properties of the individual's approach to the world. In this kind of situation also, of course, the patient's conception of the world has for him the quality of absolute reality, and the therapist's task may be to persuade him that alternatives are possible.

The measures discussed so far which people may take to increase their control over what happens to them are on the whole defensive, in the sense that they involve to some degree a retreat from anxiety-arousing circumstances. It is also, of course, possible to attempt to exercise control by more positive procedures, as for example is the case with magic. It is well recognized, for instance, that obsessional rituals frequently seem to involve an attempt to control by magic (in ways obviously analogous to religious rituals) the evil that may befall the patient or those he loves. Sometimes also obsessional rituals seem to be used by patients as a means of controlling themselves, or at least as a way of checking up on what havoc uncontrollable aspects of themselves might have wreaked while they, as it were, were not looking. Once again it is the premises on which their behaviour is based which may need to be the focus of therapeutic negotiation—the premise in particular that the world is unbearable if it cannot be controlled.

The 'game-playing' quality of the patient's behaviour is another feature which may well attract the therapist's attention. In this kind of situation it may begin to dawn on the therapist that much of the behaviour which his patient experiences as painful and barely supportable does in fact play a very positive part in helping him maintain a position of considerable psychological gain, and indeed, if it wasn't for the fact that he *suffered* for it, the manipulative aspect of the patient's behaviour would become blatantly obvious to all, including himself. Eric Berne describes a variety of such 'games' in his book (see Chapter 2), and it would be pointless to reiterate them here. In my own experience, one of the commonest, and most rewarding, games that can be played is that of victim, or martyr. Both involve suffering, and so can be expected to command respect and sympathy, and both entail a kind of unassailable moral superiority which necessarily blinds the onlooker to the fact that the victim, or martyr (once, that is, martyrdom has been achieved), has to *do* nothing further to earn respect or justify moral superiority. He has, at the expense it is true of some discomfort, arrived at a position from which he can never put a foot wrong. Here, as in the other situations discussed, it is likely to be the *meaning* of his behaviour which will become the centre of therapeutic interest: the patient may emphasize the painful and inescapable nature of his predicament, while the therapist may try to alert him to what it is doing *for* him.

If the course of negotiation has been successful, the patient may well by now be facing the prospect that his symptoms and behaviour have meanings of which he had been unaware, and yet for which he must bear the responsibility. Having gained some understanding of his situation, he is confronted by the alarming prospect of having to do something about it. In many ways this may be the most difficult and painful stage of psychotherapy.

The *painfulness* of change, the fact that the abandonment of symptoms is often accompanied by depression and despair, though by no means ignored in the therapeutic literature, seems often to surprise patients and alarm therapists, to the point that the former may break off therapy and the latter conclude that things must somewhere have gone awry. One of the central features of this pain, and one which does not seem to figure greatly in theoretical discussions known to the writer, seems to consist simply in the agony of having been *wrong*. Over and above the obvious disadvantages of losing the protection of neurotic, self-deceptive strategies, a person may feel very keenly indeed a sense of shame and wastefulness at having used them in the first place. 'Resistance' in psychotherapy is, as we have noted, most often seen as resistance to giving up neurotic symptoms and the protection they bring, but less often as resistance to other implications of changing away from neurotic strategy. To change your approach to a problem implies, however, that your former approach was wrong. And if the problem in question happens to involve almost everything your life has stood for, including the way you relate to the people in it, having been 'wrong' brings with it an infinity of—for you—shameful memories and wounding self-accusations of wasted time. Moreover, there is the added problem that you can no longer recognize yourself as the person you used to know, and there is a terrifying uncertainty about how the person you now have the opportunity of becoming behaves: you don't know what to do to be yourself.

What enables a patient to embark upon the course of accepting responsibility for himself depends presumably on a complex set of circumstances and seems to vary greatly from person to person. More often than not it seems that the process cannot be hurried. It may be the case during the earlier stages of negotiation in therapy that the therapist quite quickly sees regularities and significances in the patient's behaviour, which seem indeed extraordinarily obvious, but to which the patient remains blind despite repeated efforts from the therapist to point them out. And then one day, perhaps several months later, the patient may suddenly see the same thing that the therapist has been seeing all along. Furthermore, the patient's discovery is likely to have a very *personal* quality about it, and it is only after examining it for some time that he realizes the similarity between his discovery and what the therapist has been struggling to show him for weeks. It seems in this way often to be the case that, just as scientific or intellectual discoveries seem to follow a certain stage of development in the general cultural climate,[3] so individuals have to be in some sense 'ripe' for personal discoveries. It may be, as perhaps the non-directive approach of Rogerian client-centred therapy would suggest, that the activity itself of two people—patient and therapist—investigating seriously and in good faith the meaning of the former's situation and of the relationship between them leads to a natural 'ripening' of this kind on the patient's part. Or it may be that the therapist's persistent attempts to persuade his patient to view himself in a different light are accepted only slowly and grudgingly, but do eventually bear fruit. The result, in any case, is that therapist and patient suddenly find themselves sharing a view they formerly did not share, and it is these discoveries of commonality which afford some of the most rewarding moments in psychotherapy. Where before they had been engaged in a hard round of diplomatic—and occasionally more overtly confronting—negotiations, the two participants suddenly find themselves co-operating in an elaboration of experiences they share in common, and each is able to illuminate aspects of the situation which had, perhaps, existed for the other as no more than barely formulated questions. Like two strangers in a railway carriage who discover some personal circumstance in their background which they share, therapist and patient find themselves suddenly with a common foundation on which they can build successfully and productively. And, as a consequence, they may find that they are able to *reveal* things about themselves where before they felt a frustrated isolation.

Earlier in therapy, attempts at such self-revelation may have met with little success. It is fairly common, for example, for patients to ask the therapist to tell them 'what he thinks' of them, or in some way to expound his theoretical beliefs. Most frequently, efforts on his part to do so, however honestly undertaken and attentively received, are met with a curiously disappointed puzzlement, and consequently therapists may feel reluctant to make the attempt in the first place. This is often perceived by patients as a stubborn, mystifying secrecy on the therapist's part. From the latter's point of view, however, it may rather stem from a recognition that there is little point in laying his cards on the table until the time is ripe. The turning point may be reached in a variety of ways, but usually arises out of an actual experience the patient has undergone, perhaps within, but equally possibly outside the therapeutic situation. A young man who has for years resisted and obscured the realization of his own anger and hatred, and hedged himself around with obsessional rituals to protect himself against them, suddenly hurls a plate at his mother's head, misses, and smashes the window. Not only does he discover thereby that he *is* angry, but that he can express his anger without totally disastrous consequences, and *immediately* abandons his obsessional precautions against it. At his next therapeutic session he is able to discuss with his therapist a view of himself, and its implications, which this incident has (for him) brought to light, a view which his therapist has been trying to convince him of for months. Such discoveries may also be made in less dramatic ways.

In some ways, as has already been discussed in this book, the recognition that one has been using self-deceptive strategies in the past renders their future use impossible. (No doubt the same *behaviour* can be used, but as part of a repertoire of practised actions, not self-deceptively as the vanguard of one's activity.) This does not mean, however, that change is not hard work. It has already been suggested that to become responsible and to learn a new stance in the world demands courage. It may be that the discovery of a view of himself which he can *share* with his therapist is to an extent an encouraging experience for a patient, but he is nevertheless likely to find himself faced with burdens which only he can carry. Although the symptoms which formerly helped him to avoid the situations he most feared may have lost their centrality and importance quite early in therapy, he is still faced with having to tackle those situations. As was discussed in Chapter 5, it is at this stage in particular that the techniques devised by behaviour therapists may be helpful in encouraging the patient actively to face and challenge the feared situations.

A person's attempts at meeting situations which formerly he has dreaded and avoided may not always be attended by unqualified success. He may panic, or despair, or experience a renascence of his old symptoms. 'You have', as one patient said, 'to work at your problems *beyond* breaking point.' Fortunately, because the fears are exaggerated and the person usually stronger than he suspects, it is likely to be the problems which disintegrate rather than the person.

At this stage of psychotherapy it is likely that the therapist finds himself less in the role of negotiator, and more in that of accomplice and support. The understanding which by now he shares with his patient of the latter's position may enable him to clarify more quickly and acceptably than before the reasons for the occurrence of stumbling blocks to the patient's progress, and much of his time may be spent in simply aiding and abetting the patient's experimentation with his new stance in the world.

More or less about this time, however, one particular myth of psychotherapy may arise (though not necessarily so) to disturb the therapeutic peace. This is the myth of there being a recognizable end-point to therapy. It is again an expectation created by mechanistic thinking that there will come a point when either patient or therapist or both will recognize that the former is 'better'. It is not infrequent for a patient to ask his therapist, perhaps somewhat hesitantly, if he thinks he's better. Somehow, it seems, there must come a point when a patient is finalized as a competent, normal person. As far as the patient is concerned one of the reasons for feeling he needs this kind of reassurance may be that he doesn't particularly *feel* like an end-product. Indeed, although his symptoms may have disappeared, although he may be living in some respects a new life, doing things he has not done for years—or possibly has never done before—he may not feel 'better' at all. It may be necessary at this point for the therapist to negotiate with the patient a view of people as *not* 'better' or 'worse', 'normal' or 'abnormal', and the patient may realize that his earlier dread of his own incompetence and his fear of facing the world's demands were in part based on a false premise that 'normal' people do not have these problems. Even though, in other words, he has lost much of his former view of himself, he may not yet have abandoned entirely his former view of others, and may be waiting in vain to obtain the kind of idealized situation he imagines they occupy. In a rather similar way, it is often discouraging and disappointing for a therapist to find, despite—from his own point of view—vast improvements in a patient's symptoms and ability to cope with life, that the latter does not jump for joy and acknowledge with gratitude all that has been done for him.

This is, of course, only really a problem for patients and therapists who have accepted a model of human functioning which envisages an ideal product. It has already been suggested that successful psychotherapy can (in good faith) do no more than help free somebody to pursue their existence. It cannot guarantee a kind of painless end-state in which all life's obstacles are surmounted. Indeed, it is possible for psychotherapy to open a person's eyes to fear, despair, travail and grief, where formerly he did not see them. But at least, in *looking*, he can do something about them. The end of psychotherapy coincides more or less with the assumption of responsibility, and there is nothing *necessarily* marvellous about that; the rest of life has to be lived.

This rather sketchy outline of some of the things which might take place in the course of psychotherapy suggests, if nothing else, that a reliance on the therapist's part on some kind of technical expertise need play no very great role in psychotherapy. What is important, however, is his willingness to enter into a personal relationship with his patients, and to rely upon his personal experience in testing out his therapeutic hunches. The nature of his personal relationship with patients might vary widely; at times it may be one of struggle and confrontation, at others of encouragement and communion, but throughout it should be of the kind characterized by Martin Buber[4] as 'I-Thou' rather than 'I-It'. In other words, the therapist is, whether he likes it or not, likely to be immersed *in* the relationship, rather than standing apart from it in an analytic, calculated, categorizing way (Buber's distinction is one which has been found illuminating by many modern psychotherapists).

This does not mean that the therapist cannot or should not make use of his experience of therapy. On the contrary, much of what he does he will do in the light of previous experience, and his perception of what happens in any particular psychotherapeutic encounter will inevitably be shaped by his experience of earlier ones. Indeed, it is this experience more than anything else which qualifies him to be considered a professional psychotherapist. This experience is, however, personal, rooted in his own history and his own activity; it does not have to seek authority from any impersonal objectivity of the sort beloved of 'behavioural scientists'.

As has been argued before, the instrument whereby the therapist understands his patients is none other than himself. The argument for this view, in the slightly different but related context of social psychology, has been well put by Harré and Secord:[5]

We believe that a human being is a system of a different *order* of complexity from any other existing system, natural or artificial. We believe this to be evident in the fact of human self-awareness and in the characteristically human linguistic powers. Thus for the purposes of any science which deals with phenomena specifically associated with performances that depend upon these higher order capacities any model of less complexity is void. Thus, machines, computers in their present state of development, and animals, are *all* inadequate, though none are wholly useless, as sources for concepts with which to delineate a sufficiently powerful model of man, which can be of any real use 'in the scientific understanding of social phenomena. The only possible solution is to use our understanding of ourselves as the basis for the understanding of others, and our understanding of others of our species to further our understanding of ourselves.

The therapist's richest source of information about what goes on in people is what goes on in himself. To accept, elaborate, and build upon this is to be scientific, in the sense in which that term has been developed in this book.

In his understanding of others, no one has in any case the possibility of being anything but personal in his approach, and hence subjective. This is, however, the special kind of subjectivity which can be shared and developed with others, not the inflexible, dogmatic, opinionated subjectivity which is often contrasted with an 'enlightened', impersonal objectivity. Perhaps, indeed, dogmatic subjectivity fulfils a useful purpose as a defence against the crushing weight of impersonal objectivity as the latter is used as a 'scientific' cudgel, but since we have abandoned the latter, we have no need of the former. Our task, whether therapists or patients (or scientists), is to investigate and negotiate the degree to which our subjectivities overlap.

The psychotherapist who chooses to ignore his experience of himself when trying to understand his patients may end up weaving theories or building psychological models which are likely to be remarkable, to the unclouded eye, only for their banality and conspicuous lack of truth, even though they may well be accepted by that section of the intellectual (or indeed wider) community which has a vested interest in 'objectivity' and mechanism. Ultimately, this is likely to lead to a view of patients' experience and, more particularly, behaviour as intrinsically meaningless.

At the risk of labouring an example used earlier in this book, let us take once again the case of a young woman who complains of 'frigidity'. She has, she says, lost all interest in sex, and cannot bear her husband to touch her, although he is a 'good husband' and she loves him. Now there are several ways in which the professional helper might approach her problem. The 'objective' approach (probably that most frequently taken by psychiatrists and psychologists, in Britain at least) is to accept the complaint as a *datum* in this patient's situation. The problem then becomes one of *reinstating* her sexual response, either mechanically by juggling in some way with her anatomy or body chemistry, or by means of some kind of 'retraining' method using conditioning procedures. Explanations of her condition likely to be invoked will in all probability be in terms of 'the physiology of the human sexual response' or of a mechanistic behavioural psychology. When she says she 'hates to be touched', this is more likely to be understood as a description of an inappropriate sensation than as an experience carrying *meaning*, and as a consequence will be taken as an indication of (almost literally) her wires having got crossed in some way, rather than as a statement about her relationship with her husband which should be taken seriously.

If, on the other hand, the therapist looks within himself for some strand of his experience which resonates in sympathy with the patient's complaint, he may find the beginnings of an understanding which can be formed with her about what it *means*. He may, for example, *know* what it is like not to like being touched, and he may be aware of his reasons, in the past perhaps, for not having liked being touched, and he may speculate that his patient may have similar reasons of which, however, she is unaware. It is at this point that he must avoid the errors of a negative subjectivity. He must not, that is, assume that this woman's reasons for disliking being touched *must* be the same as his, and he must not consequently insist, more or less subtly, that she accept his version of the state of affairs. Instead, through the process of negotiation, he should test the correctness of his hypothesis by helping her to elaborate her own meanings and to find out where they end up; in this aspect, negotiation is very similar to scientific experiment. The importance of his own experience in this kind of situation lies in making the formation of hypotheses possible. The ensuing procedure of negotiation will determine how much therapist and patient do share in the experience of disliking being touched, but in any case may allow the latter to discover for herself what disliking being touched means to her. The reciprocity of negotiation is again well stated by Harré and Secord:[6]

When we try to persuade the person to 'see' his situation differently, to attend to other aspects of a situation than those he was considering, and so on, we are trying to change the meaning of the situation for him. We try to get him to ascribe different meanings to things and situations from those he ascribed before which influenced his past choice of mentalistic predicates. If this is true, it must be possible for our subject to counter-persuade us to see the matter his way too.

It seems obvious that the likely outcomes of the 'objective' approach on the one hand, and the 'subjective' approach on the other, will be different. In the first case, the woman in question will find herself the harbinger of a 'sexual dysfunction' which may or may not be improved by mechanical intervention, but which will enable her to persist in her relationship with her husband much as before, in the role of faulty (or repaired) machine. In the second case, the patient may arrive at a reformulation of her position, in which disliking being touched means something about her relationship with her husband—e.g. that, in some sense at least, she does *not* love him and see him as a 'good husband', and has reasons for not doing so. These reasons could of course be of widely differing kinds, ranging from her own expectations of what a husband should be (which her husband cannot live up to), to her husband's expectations of what a wife should be (which she cannot accept). Whatever the final outcome for their relationship—whether divorce or an idyllic sex life—she will at least be permitted the role of a fully functioning person.

The 'subjective' approach is, then, made possible by the therapist's determination not to depart from an understanding of the situation which is rooted in his own experience. For him, 'not liking to be touched' has a *meaning* (in personal terms) which he is not willing to abandon in favour of a *meaningless*, abstract notion of 'sexual dysfunction' which appeals to some kind of unknown physical or behavioural pathology.

Without *some* basis in common experience, understanding between therapist and patient is impossible, for each remains an enigma to the other. This does not, on the other hand, necessarily mean that one can only understand and communicate with people whose problems and experiences are identical to one's own. As suggested in the previous chapter, it may still be possible for two people to learn about each other through a reciprocal master-apprentice relationship in which each starts from the position that the other's experience is valid. Even so, some initial overlap in experience is essential, and it may well be true that the more patient and therapist share in terms of experience, the more possible it will be for them to develop a therapeutic understanding. This would perhaps seem obvious if it was not so often overlooked. It is surprising how often one will find on the therapeutic scene unmarried marital counsellors, childless child psychotherapists, and in general therapists attempting to deal with situations—for example, death and bereavement—of which they have no personal experience. In the case of such fundamental human experiences as these, theoretical knowledge is but a pale substitute for personal familiarity with them. In order to understand the significance of an individual's heart sounds, a physician must have a background of experience in listening to such sounds—a mere description in a book, in the absence of actual experience, would tell him nothing about this individual. Similarly, it is impossible for somebody who has not experienced the state of marriage, of parenthood, or the event of death, to develop the necessary standards by which to judge the experience of others in these respects. These are experiences 'the want of which', as Kant put it, 'no scholastic discipline can compensate'.

Rather than a therapist's credentials reflecting a certified training in a particular theory, or the acquisition of a set of pseudo-technical skills, the above observations seem to move us towards judging his worth by appeal to the width of (and his sensitivity to) his personal experience.

This may in many ways seem an alarming prospect. It is impossible to see how therapeutic brass plates could either honestly or succinctly give an account of their owner's breadth or depth of experience, or his qualities as a person, and in any case one imagines that in no time at all the kind of sickening shorthand description which comes to be imposed on people in this sort of context ('Great Human Being') would be institutionalized in the form of training and the award of certificates and degrees.

But if we are to take seriously the *personal* nature of psycho-therapeutic activity, and if we reject the professional mystification of psychotherapy by appeal to the acquisition of certain technical skills, or indoctrination in a particular therapeutic approach, then we must at least attempt to formulate an alternative. The tempta-tion here, as ever, is to buttress a personal stance by reinforcing it with some kind of impersonal criterion which will carry with it the authority of 'reality'—i.e. to formulate general standards to be met by psychotherapists, without regard to the fact that they are individuals. We can perhaps at least in part avoid doing this by appealing once more to the notion of social negotiation. Who is to be accounted a 'competent' psychotherapist will be a matter for negotiation, and not of objective criterion. There may be certain aspects of his activity which a psychotherapist can appeal to in order to differentiate himself from, for example, faith healers, well-meaning friends or out-and-out charlatans. He may, for instance, have a commitment to make what he does public, and to expose its intellectual foundations; he may point to the length of his experience, and convey the dedication and seriousness with which he views it and reflects upon it. He may, in other words, point to aspects of his activity which at least *provide a context for* the development of personal understanding of therapeutic issues. But in no way can he *guarantee* that he has indeed developed such understanding. No matter how great his age or experience, how long his training or the string of letters after his name, his worth and wisdom as a therapist will either emerge or evaporate anew in each individual therapeutic relationship.

This is not to say, however, that the issue of professional accreditation can safely be disregarded. Patients have a right to know whether their potential therapists have at least been exposed to the kind of experience likely to make them competent, and whether or not they are so considered by their colleagues. Unlike many other professional guilds, in which the competence of an individual member may be judged by reference to the quality of his work, psychotherapeutic organizations can unfortunately offer little in the way of reassurance to prospective consumers. This is partly because of the difficulties involved in demonstrating that psychotherapy 'works', but even more perhaps because of the theoretical dogmas which divide psychotherapists. Such divisions tend to focus therapists' attention on demonstrating suitably strong allegiance to a particular dogma in order to be admitted to this or that therapeutic club, rather than on developing a personal understanding of therapy which may be shared with others. Before this problem can be resolved, therapists of all persuasions may have to spend more time in elaborating their actual experience of psychotherapy, and less in trying to force their experience to fit preconceived notions of what will make them respectable in the eyes of the 'scientific' orthodoxy.

The fact that he can in the last analysis rely on little more than his personal resources (and accepting that psychotherapy is a fundamentally personal relationship) means that the therapist may well have to come to terms with certain limitations on his activities. For reasons which have been discussed above—reasons, that is, which have their origin in the nature and extent of his personal experience and familiarity with certain kinds of human situations and conditions—he may find that there are people he cannot help. There may, for example, be people who are wrestling with problems of which he has no conception, or whose personal development far outstrips anything he has encountered. In such cases it may well be wiser for him to recognize the hopelessness of being able to form a useful therapeutic relationship with the person concerned than to rely on technical expertise to pull him through any situation. If he is misled by some notion of professional expertise into feeling duty-bound to take on such patients for therapy, he may well find the therapeutic roles being reversed, so that he learns more from his patient than the latter from him. Of course, if he is able to acknowledge this state of affairs, then no harm may be done, and indeed the experience may prove mutually enriching for both, but it seems on the whole more likely that he will find himself becoming increasingly anxious and self-doubting, perhaps falling back on mystifying professional authority which can only impair the relationship and bewilder the patient.

This does not mean that the therapist has in some way to be morally superior to his patients, but merely that there may be some situations in which he is unlikely to be of much help to them. If, for example, a therapist is engaged in the same kind of self-deceptive strategies as his patient, it is likely that they will reinforce each other's problems rather than resolve them. Having said this, however, one has to recognize that (apart, possibly, from a feeling of happy unanimity which the participants may experience) there are no objective criteria by means of which the presence of such a state of affairs can be recognized. The main safeguard, perhaps, would be the existence of a psychotherapeutic community which acknowledges the personal nature of therapy and which affords the individual therapist opportunities for consultation, discussion, support and supervision.

In my anxiety to represent psychotherapy as a fundamentally personal undertaking, I do not wish to suggest that questions either of technique or of theoretical study are anathema, or even merely irrelevant. The psychotherapeutic literature, in all its aspects, is a rich source of ideas concerning ways in which therapeutic 'movement' may be achieved, negotiations initiated, and patients encouraged to cope with their problems. What I am concerned to stress is that such ideas and techniques can only operate flexibly in the context of a personal relationship, and carry no guarantee of success as purely mechanical ways of changing people. There is, moreover, nothing sacrosanct about them, nothing which justifies their becoming the patented property of any particular group or profession: they can be effective only as they are freely adapted to the needs of each particular therapeutic situation. It is, of course, essential for the psychotherapist to be well versed in the intellectual problems as well as the therapeutic efforts and achievements of the professional community to which he belongs, just so long as he does not attempt to turn his knowledge into a mystique and convert his profession, or a section of it, into some kind of élite magic circle.

It will certainly be feared by many that any conceptualization of psychotherapy along the lines of that offered here, if accepted, would destroy all possibility of conducting rewarding research work in this area. All possibility of making and communicating findings of lasting worth becomes lost, it might be felt, in an infinitely variable sea of individual and personal bits and pieces of experience. Orthodox methods of psychological research, it might be argued, even though they may not have advanced our understanding of psychology very far, at least contain the *possibility* of so doing, whereas to accept the formulation offered here would be to abandon all hope and to consign the entire field to the individual whims and impulses of its practitioners. I feel myself, however, that the very reverse might be the case.

It is true that acceptance of a view of psychotherapy as *personal* leads to very different kinds of research strategy from those to be found in orthodox approaches, but it may well be the case that psychological *understanding* will be greatly increased by departure from orthodoxy. We may, of course, have to sacrifice prediction, control and 'general laws' to such understanding, but, because these are in any case in principle unattainable, the loss is really no loss at all.

As a first step, we may agree with Harré and Secord[7] that:

The processes that are productive of social behaviour occur in individual people, and it is in individual people that they must be studied. It is here that the vitally important dimensions of spontaneity and idiosyncrasy occur. To achieve full scientific status, then, social psychology must make room for attempts to unravel the modes of generation of social behaviour 'within' the person. And this can be achieved only from the basis of an intensive study of particular cases, in which one may hope to discern the productive and generative 'mechanisms' at work, such as the evaluation of reasons, the making concordant of beliefs, and so on. It is precisely this kind of study that the statistical method makes impossible, since it is concerned to eliminate idiosyncratic features of people by the use of controls, and by the method of random assignment to classes. This is usually coupled with the assumption that changes produced externally and extrinsically to a person are determinative of his performance, attitudes, and so on, an assumption which effectively eliminates the dimension of spontaneity, and the vitally important capacity to consciously monitor performances, which is very characteristic of human behaviour and plays a very large role in determining the form the reactions take. It is in the detailed study of particular cases that we shall make progress towards discerning the patterns of reasons, feelings, beliefs, impulses, and so on that are responsible for the external relations and overall patterns discerned by the use of the statistical method.

It is also possible to go a step further and to suggest that, as far as psychotherapy is concerned (and many other psychological situations, come to that), the very procedure itself *is* psychological research, and its usefulness as such, as well as its communicability, will depend on a recognition of its personal nature and the consequent development of a language of common experience, and a fundamental attitude of good faith towards that experience, in which its findings can be shared and elaborated.

Psychological research then becomes a *co-operative* venture, in which both psychologist and subject (or therapist and patient) attempt to realize the scientific aim, rather than (as it has been in recent decades) a *competitive* situation in which psychologist tries to outwit subject, or trick him into revealing in an unguarded moment something about himself which can in any case be of only fleeting interest.

Indeed, orthodox research procedures often seem to be almost perversely aimed at obscuring important matters of psychological interest. This is achieved, as has been said, partly through the use of a methodology which is concerned with measurement for its own sake rather than with the phenomena which present themselves in the research worker's experience, and partly through a widespread obsession with generalities. Many psychiatric patients, for example, are able to give the interested inquirer quite fascinating insights into their (often very individual) experiences of physical treatment methods such as electro-convulsive therapy and the use of tranquillizers and anti-depressants. A patient may describe, for instance, the generally blunting effect that tranquillizers have had on his perception of the world around him—the whole of his experience becoming dulled, and not just his anxiety. (One man who of his own accord gave up his tablets had to shut his clock in a cupboard as its ticking had suddenly become unbearably loud.) Again, anti-depressants may make a person feel more cheerful, but without his knowing why: he has a kind of chemical euphoria which is unrelated to the events which happen to him, and which is thus a source of an entirely new kind of confusion. The use of questionnaires or other standardized, 'reliable' and 'valid' measures of mood or ability, averaged out across an inevitably heterogeneous population, make it extremely unlikely that, for example, a useful phenomenology of drug usage could be elaborated. A personal, co-operative exploration of a patient's experience of drugs in relation to his individual problems and difficulties might do much more to achieve a genuinely scientific understanding of the factors involved.

In some ways, then, psychotherapy, in the sense in which it has been treated here, can be taken as a model of psychological research rather than just another field of study for it. If as the result we have to do without the security and authority of an (illusory) impersonal objectivity, we may at least find ourselves with the opportunity of sharing a common basis in experience on which to build a developing understanding of our own nature.

1 See for example a useful paper on this subject by J. Steiner, M. Jarvis and J. Parrish. (1970). Risk taking and arousal regulation. *British Journal of Medical Psychology*, **43**, 333.
2 Scott, R. D. and Ashworth, P. L. (1967). 'Closure' at the first schizophrenic break-down: a family study. *British Journal of Medical Psychology*, **40**, 109.
3 Arthur Koestler, in his book *The Act of Creation* documents particularly convincingly the way in which cultural or scientific developments take place (often independently) when the time is ripe.
4 Buber, M. (1958). *I and Thou*. Edinburgh: Clark.
5 Harre, R. and Secord, P. F. (1972). *The Explanation of Social Behaviour*, p. 87. Oxford: Blackwell.
6 ibid., p. 113.
7 ibid., p. 134.

Index

Index

Page references in italics refer to names in the endnotes to chapters.